Mama on a Mission

Voice Empowerment

Creative Writing

The Joy of Play

Sound Healing

Life Coaching

Nutrition

Yoga

Mama on a Mission

Inspired by

Laura Topper

with guest contributors

Zoë Owl ~ Belle Amatt ~ Patricia Iris Kerins

Yvonne Skelly ~ Mel Campbell

Kate Bartram Brown

Published by Laura Topper, Sacred Path Publishing © 2016

Sussex, England

Mama on a Mission
Published in the United Kingdom 2016
by Sacred Path Publishing

www.lauratopper.com

Cover art by Jim Warren www.jimwarren.com

Graphics by Aaron Austin Locke

Editorial services by Dawn ProofPerfect
www.dawnproofperfect.co.uk

ISBN 9 781782 809821

I AM SO VERY GRATEFUL to all of the women authors contributing in this book and also to Dawn Austin Locke for her loving care and wisdom in giving this book roots to ground and wings to fly... Thank you,

Laura

PELE – HAWAIIAN VOLCANO & FIRE GODDESS

PELE, THE FIRE GODDESS, embodies dynamic creativity, fiery passion, birth and rebirth. Pele reminds us of our ability to transcend that which does not serve us well, allowing the innate creative force within to manifest our heart's desires with love, passion and most importantly, affirmative action. Pele embodies the divine feminine at its very best – beautiful, creative, powerful, capable of all possibility – demonstrating strength of conviction combined with dignity, love and compassion. Pele challenges us to remember how the divine feminine can and will change the world around us for the better in a loving, powerful, sacred and compassionate way. Are you ready for her challenge?

Yvonne Skelly

THANK YOU JIM…

I am so grateful to award-winning artist Jim Warren for gifting the empowered cover image of *Pele Rising* as the eternal message of strength and knowing for all women on their mission

Laura

CONTENTS

MANDALAS Fourteen mandalas are lovingly included between chapters to allow you to pause for thought as you connect from one written piece to the next. Meditate on them or colour them creatively and freely.

Dreamtime mandala

INTRODUCTION

Heather Andrews-Dobbs

I was delighted to become acquainted with seven beautiful, empowered soul sisters who have contributed to *Mama on a Mission* when leading New Thought pioneer, Laura Topper, sent me extracts of the book she has co-created. What a fabulous project! These wonderful women, have bared and shared their explorations, trials and enlightened insights with us. I am sure that as you joyously leaf through these pages you will connect with those women as soul sisters and friends, you will find aspects of their journey is your journey – those pivotal moments that nudge you to reclaim your power and reconnect with your authentic self. Whatever we experience in this 3D world, our soul prompts us towards our potential – greater freedom, fun, laughter, wisdom and love.

The Dalai Lama once said, 'The world will be saved by Western women'. His statement ignites a flame in the hearts of all awakened Divine Mamas! Take courage, step forward, come out of the shadows and shine your light! It is through the awakening of each individual that the world can awaken. Women are being called to provide a more feminine type of leadership in all sectors of society, be it healthcare, education, politics or governance. The Dalai Lama was aware that Western women don't face the same obstacles of oppression as experienced in many other cultures. We are coming towards the end of women being marginalised.

If we allow the Divine to flow through us we can take our rightful place in society, co-creating a world based on divine principles and replacing the current oppressive system of human rights. It is time to have women pioneering new ways of cooperative leadership in the world.

I recall the late Anita Roddick, founder of The Body Shop, speaking at a conference on Consciousness at the

Alternatives centre, Piccadilly, London some years ago. During the conference Anita suggested that it was time for the world to be run by 'postmen or pausal women'! Perplexed looks registered on the faces of the audience. After a few seconds the penny dropped – she was suggesting that the world was run by post-menopausal women! Women have a natural slant towards compassion, kindness cooperation and equanimity; these are the values that will prevent humankind destroying itself through wars and competition.

Visualise a bright light between yourself and Source. This light starts to energise and glow radiantly, bringing the infinite power of Source which is working through you. Now call upon the Goddesses to help you ascend and fulfil your Soul mission. Quan Jin is radiating her light down to Earth spreading divine feminine energy to empower women and help men get more in touch with their feminine side. The Divine Mother is on a mission and we, her daughters, are on a mission too. How exciting!

Heather Andrews-Dobbs, New Thought Minister

Winner of three International Golden Heart Inspiration Awards.

Contact: www.everythingforthegoddess.com

DEDICATION

Mama on a Mission is lovingly devoted to all women around the world, thank you for your inspiration and for being the reason for this book.

Mama on a Mission

Planting Seeds

Laura Topper

I SAT IN MY PRAYER ROOM AT HOME just after Christmas this year, really feeling ready to share my knowing, along with six other inspired authors, with women globally; to inspire others to just BE the beauty and magnificence that they already are. Having journeyed so far, I wondered what it would feel like for women to have a book handy on the kitchen table bringing together seven devoted women's honest perspectives of continuing with their dreams, desires and highest visions for their life, regardless of the so-called obstacles and daily challenges of harmonising life, families, children, dream-believing, creativity, fun and play. My inspiration and intention for writing *Mama on a Mission* and calling in these glorious women who I have encountered over the past three years, Patricia Iris Kerins, Belle Amatt, Zoë Owl, Mel Campbell, Yvonne Skelly, Kate Bartram Brown and Heather Andrews-Dobbs, is to inspire and enable you to know that you *can have it all*. But, one key thing goes along with having it all and that is knowing that you already *are it all*, right here and right now. You need do no more than embrace your magnificence, your light, the energy of love, and to live your life from a place of deep *inner power* which can then only ripple out of your heart into your relationships, your creativity, your work, your children and your world around you. It all begins with you and it's your choice. I can assure you that as healers, teachers, coaches, creatives, mothers, lovers and everyday women, we have each been through and still are on our own journeys of testing times and challenges. We know first-hand the road of self-commitment, patience, self love and gratitude and are oozing with information, tools and techniques for you to place into your life, right *here* and right *now*, to inspire you to a deep inner knowing of yourself as the empowered and loving light you already are; in an instant of choice, you can flick the switch to being it all.

I am so blessed that the women I embrace into this book, are those forging their path with love and absolute faith and as I asked each one of them to contribute to my idea, they each proclaimed 'Yes!' with a beaming smile of excitement and joy. And on top of it all we have the blessing of Heather Andrews-Dobbs with her Goddess-inspired words of wisdom at the beginning of the book.

It is no coincidence that you are drawn to reading *Mama on a Mission.* This book is here for you at whatever point you are in your life, simply because you are here *now* and have taken time to read this far... The exercises and tools are simple for those who are new to self-development and also refreshing for those more used to life coaching and inner work. As you read through and take in both the inner-world steps and tangible tools that I, and the other authors, offer you can begin from where you are, in the here and now, to put our suggestions into your life. The beauty of this is that, as you begin, you are consciously saying 'Yes!' to opening up to wondrous opportunities that await you and bold possibilities that you could only dream of. Take this book as a loving friend for your life, for this moment; for you to take the seeds that you know are in your heart and to nurture, water, love, feed and grow them, knowing they are your oak trees, which are becoming within you.

As we each learn to master our lives, the so-called obstacles, the highs and lows, harmonising with ourselves, our partners and lovers, families and friends and with our children too, it can be so empowering to turn to a book that is written with love from knowing and experience by women who are, as you are, living in the midst of life and who are able to inspire and share with you the deeper teachings that push us on in persistence and faith. Our message to you is loud and clear, one of love, acceptance and a deep knowing, to inspire you to believe in yourself and live in the deeper faith that *you are enough*. It is our deepest intention that you become aware of your beauty and shine your own light with self-confidence, self-acceptance and, above all, unconditional self love. Enjoy the ride and get ready for inner transformation.

Take a full breath
and know
you are
MORE THAN ENOUGH

You certainly are enough just as you are... and *Mama on a Mission* is here for you as a dynamic reinforcement to remind you that, whoever you are, whatever you are going through, however you perceive your situation, however tough you think things are, you always have choice. Yes, you can choose to live from fear, 'What if?' and 'I can't!' and 'I'm not good enough.' that's certainly a choice! Or you can enable that higher, empowered place of loving and accepting yourself and the situation, and live in the knowing that you *are enough*, just as you are. You are here to be the magnificence of all you are and to express this fully in life, right now, from the place of love that includes loving YOU, your self, just as you are.

Your Inner Mission

As we peel away the layers of doubt and fear, we are brought into bareness, to embrace and live our lives fully-expressed and have complete faith in the limitless supply of all the abundant good that exists; we can be supported by life with each and every loving step we take. For me, being on a mission is not about focusing on what I am doing *out there* in the world. What it's really all about is my inner mission to learn, more deeply, ways to love myself, accept myself, to live from my inner power, to forgive and live in the flow of all good; to be grateful for all I'm experiencing, even things I can't understand and don't like, and to know above everything that I am loved and accepted unconditionally by life itself. I am enough as love. Wow, what a code to crack! This is my mission. I LOVE IT and have devoted many years to its fine tuning; I invite you to embrace and live your inner mission right now: to see and feel life and all its miracles and to allow love to guide your way.

So Far So Good

We are constantly facing messages of lack, surrounding us from all angles, from the media and everyday life: there's not enough, could be better, could look better, could do better. The choice we have is whether we decide to acknowledge these false claims or to rise up and play the game of life from a space of being enough, from our Goddess place of power, creating and living life through knowing that the thoughts we choose to replay, over and over, create our personal world. It's no surprise that our perception of life is marred by subliminal messages which we unknowingly take on board. One message that women are fed is that we are not capable of overcoming what lies before us and are victims, powerless to step into the strength of who we really are – that we have to 'juggle' to live the life of our dreams; this is a message I would like to rub out and delete from all time consciousness. Women have travelled a warrior path since time began to arrive where we are today, with our roles redefined again and again. Even in the past hundred years our priorities have shifted from women tying themselves to railings for the vote, to being the post-war woman at home, moving on to becoming go-getter and breadwinner while our men are re-roled into house husbands. Then we shifted to being creative Earth Mothers, living in the essence of creative expression, and forward to lone mum, working hard to survive and not feeling great. The latest version of woman is a 'whateverpreneur', here to change the world from a (no pressure) 0-6 figure salary in two weeks and serve three-course meals at the same time. We are so much stronger and more creative than even we give ourselves credit for.

Wow, how things have shifted in this century! Or have they? Who are we as women, mothers, creative spirits, entrewhatevers and lovers? What outrageous expectations do we place on ourselves to be perfect when, in spiritual truth, we already are? How are we coping as women in our self-designed consciousness of needing to have it, do it and be it, all at the same time? Surely it's time to take a big step back and *feel* what we are living and know that, as individuals, we can choose to understand that we're already complete and to feel empowered by this? So, how far have we really come in the past hundred years? We remain in a web of unequal wage, just for being women. I know we certainly have more say, more choice, possibly more sexual power, more freedom and some equality, but do we really use our inner wisdom and power in the wisest way, to embrace and empower a deep knowing of fully loving and accepting ourselves? I think not; this is where there is great work to be done and I know you agree, simply because you are here, now, reading *Mama on a Mission*. Welcome home, you've arrived safely!

So, our BIG message and intention is to bring you to your own *knowing* that you are enough already. Yes, you are the captain of your ship and the skipper, first mate and chef – and, by the way, the first class passenger. It's up to you how you envision yourself, either as a *victim*, feeling that life is not treating you fairly and there's always something to moan about, or as a *victor*, seeing life as a huge opportunity to learn, grow and unfold with gratitude. It's that simple and it's vital for you to know you can harness and embrace the powerful tools offered here and just get on with the business of being *you*. There is choice in each moment and day and from within, all is changeable. If you feel your passion changes or that you aren't fully engaging in life for some reason, then it's time to let go of an old way, to trust the process and to move on to a new way of thinking and being – and this is okay. It's the beautiful gift of having free will and creative expression; allowing yourself to grow, expand, to discover yourself and your passions with love. Of course, there will always be perceived obstacles on the path, and those exist for us to grow from, but once you commit to you and your dreams and go for it, you can diffuse these blocks with love and see them as powerful tools for unfolding growth.

My commitment to life is to love myself unconditionally, to be the best mum that I can be, and my biggee is to transform self-worth consciousness on this planet through my songs and knowing. My passion as a singer, songwriter and spiritual teacher is firmly woven into my message for us to live life from the power of realising our worth. I know there are many things for me to learn and flourish from and I accept that as the glorious journey of my life. Many times I've been howling on the kitchen floor in lack of faith and drifted away from knowing my truth as love, but when I return to a centred place of trusting in life, I continue, with that love seeding a way before me. Finding and living with inner harmony and peace is, I believe, our individual responsibility and duty to ourselves. It's not someone else's dream: our parents, partner, ancestors, teachers, the neighbour. It's your life and it matters and counts more than anything – living it with love, faith and passion is your sweet gift.

Your New Mantra

I Am Enough

I Am Enough

I Am Enough

I Am Enough

I Am MORE THAN Enough

Being fully open in spirit, mind and body is a vital part of putting this understanding into practice and now Mel Campbell so perfectly offers her wisdom for embodying this connection.

Tree of life mandala

Passage of Time

Mel Campbell

I AM NO GURU. I AM NO EXPERT. I HAVE NO FIX. What I am is just an ordinary mum, who was invited to write a chapter for this book and to share with you. I have been married for nearly twenty years, I have three children of 17, 15 and 7 years old. I have a dog, have downsized due to too many risks and mistakes. Have loved, lost and lived.

I slam doors, I shout at my kids, I get cross, I cry and scream out of frustration. I am rubbish at cooking, I cram too much in to my already ridiculously congested schedule and it's taken me years to find myself. I am now forty-six years old.

For decades I never felt connected with myself and lived my life through the heritage of my mother, my grandmother and all that went on before me. My mother shouted at us as kids, slammed doors, threw our toys and even chased my dad up the stairs with a frying pan out of frustration, tiredness and desperation. My mother had so many secrets that I knew nothing about, could only guess at, yet I held them in my heart, in my soul and in my being. I wasn't a victim, only a victim to myself. A victim because I had never empowered myself to be free, free of all the baggage that had been passed onto me, free of the stories, judgements I had planted upon myself which had grown into knotweed that entwines itself around all the pretty flowers and wild bushes in your garden and when you get rid of some, it just keeps reappearing. I had never given myself time to be free or allowed myself to have faith in me being *me*. Come on, as women do we ever allow ourselves? We rush around trying to prove ourselves in whatever form it may be. Cramming the screaming toddlers into the car so we can rush them from one activity to another – practising their piano homework late at night so they pass their grades. Yet, who are we doing it for? Personally, I did it for me. To prove to myself I could do it. To prove to myself Iwas a good mother, yet rarely did I feel like one. Internally, I felt frustrated and impatient as a mother. Didn't love myself or honour who I was and felt annoyed with the world.

Yoga came into my life, or I into the life of yoga, when I was a mum at home with my two young children. My husband was working in London, working and playing hard. His brother had recently been murdered in the atrocities of 9/11. He was drinking lots and not coming home for nights at a time. I spent many hours sobbing on our stairs in the early mornings, then quickly wiping the tears away, as I greeted my sleepy children wandering downstairs weary-eyed. I was searching, searching for answers and searching for myself, whom I had misplaced over the months and years since entering motherhood. I became curious about yoga. It hinted at something mysterious, intriguing and unknown to me. I felt drawn to it as something I wanted to explore, so I rang a local class and asked, 'Is it fast?' because I felt I wanted to push myself. Only now do I realise after years of practising and sharing my practice, that our practice on the mat is a reflection of what we do off the mat. Ironic really, here I was a mother of two, struggling to find a minute to myself, with a husband, who worried me relentlessly and I wanted to push myself more!

Although I went to several classes it didn't draw me in, however I felt drawn to find out more. What about yoga was so seductive, entrancing? Surely it wasn't just about the odd shaped poses that decorate the covers of magazines? There must be more to it. Compelled to discover answers, I ventured on a teacher training course. Our house was on the market, we were moving to Asia, I had a business event looming and I was signing up for more. Here I was again, pushing myself even further.

I had no intentions of becoming a yoga teacher, it was more about fulfilling my curiosity and the only way was to dive in. So I embarked on the four-month course, commuting from London at the weekends, leaving my children, as I listened to my heart, one of the greatest gifts this ancient tradition has taught me. As I listened to my heart I found peace. Peace from the murder of my brother-in-law, a friend who had been in my life since I was seventeen, and the impact this was having on me and my family. The more I felt at peace with myself the more I learnt to feel at peace with others and with my world.

Yoga means 'union.' The union of the divine self with the infinite spirit. It is a practice renowned for its blending of *asanas* (poses), *pranayama* (breathing exercises) and *savasana* (relaxation), which when combined, evoke a deep meditative state which has both psychological and physiological influences on our mind, body and spirit, leaving its imprint.

For many it is so personal that it's hard to describe. It is more of an inner revelation, a feeling that seeps into your being. Slowly the knotweed peeled itself away, as I began to slow down, listen and connect with myself, my breath and my feelings. The more I practise yoga, I realise how the invented chronicles of myself that I had conceived and concocted begin to shred away and, underneath those layers, I appreciate the truth of who I really am; the essence of my being, that somehow had become murky and lost in the passage of time.

And so, my love affair with yoga began.

I Invite You to Step Into Inner Wonderland

- ♥ *For the next few minutes I invite you to stop. Read through before beginning. Fold over the corner of this page and breathe.*
- ♥ *Find a seated comfortable position where you can resist temptation to move for a few minutes. Now take a breath.*
- ♥ *Breathe in and out through your nose. Notice your breath. Take your time. No rush.*

- *Follow your inhalations and your exhalations. Merge into this rhythm as you become at one with your breath.*
- *Stay here, following your inhalations and exhalations. Take your time. No rush. Stay here for several minutes. Observing your breath and befriending it.*
- *Now begin to acknowledge your mind. Notice how you're feeling; in your mind, your body and your breath.*

The practice of Yoga invites us to take time out of our day to reconnect with ourselves, to take a breath, to feel our body and to find space between the busyness of our thoughts.

As busy mothers how often do we give ourselves permission to do this? Yet, we often hear ourselves saying, 'Oh, give me a minute to myself, please', as someone rattles at the bathroom door just as we have sat down. We may even sneak in there under the pretence that we need to go, when in actual fact we are trying to claim some moments to ourselves. We are selfless by nature, yet we struggle with a constant barrage of guilt and notions of selfishness if we seek to retrieve time to ourselves.

The following scene was played out on a famous soap drama on television:

'Where's Mum?'

'She's in the back having a few moments to herself, if she doesn't get it she'll be chasing it all day!'

That is how it feels! So often we try to hold onto a thought, as we rush down the street with bags of shopping, juggling the screaming kids who don't want to get in the buggy, yet we are in a rush and our patience is running thin as we try to hold to that thought before we forget it.

As a busy mum, it is important to claim moments for ourselves and yoga gives you the platform to do it. It sets the scene for the day, gives you *a peace of mind*, a place to feel at one with your world and all that is going on. As you step on the mat it is a declaration to yourself to step away from what has gone on before and what will go on afterwards, allowing you to delve into the moment and be fully present. It offers clarity about who we are, as we gently move away from our external into our *internal* world and feel that inner connection to ourselves.

A Peace of Mind

- *I offer you this moment to pause. Find a comfortable sitting position, close your eyes and take a breath.*
- *Connect with the rhythm of your breath. Don't think about it. Don't judge it. Just breathe.*
- *Follow your inhalations and exhalations. Notice the pauses at the end of your inhalations and exhalations. Inhale. Gentle pause. Exhale. Gentle pause.*
- *Focus awareness on the pause at the end of your exhalation. Feel the depth of this pause. Its expanse. Allow yourself to recline more completely into the pause, as if you were falling back into the arms of a loved one.*
- *Stay here for a few minutes, immersing yourself in the pause. Let your breath flow of its own accord, as you linger here in this space of stillness. Hold onto it as you slowly open your eyes back into your world.*

This is where the practice really begins. Trying to hold onto to the stillness, quietness and suspend yourself in a state of tranquillity amidst the ongoing demands of motherhood. Just as we learnt to watch and witness the breath flow freely, coming and going whilst we resided in the pause between the new breath arriving, we can learn to find the peace and calm instants between the chaotic requests of motherhood. As we held the space between each breath, feeling the depth and breadth of the pause, it began to feel expansive and spacious, despite being transient.

Take this gift with you now, practise immersing yourself in the pauses between requests and the relentless tug-of-war of motherhood. In the brief moments you have of being still and quiet, feel them, touch them and allow yourself to surrender into them. Be aware of the space around you and within you, seizing it in your heart and your being. This is the practice and yoga offers us the stage to rehearse. As we come onto our mat it becomes the reflection of who we are. As we reconnect with our breath and bodies we see and feel who we are. We touch our soul, our spirit, our being who we are. Let that leave its imprint as you step off the mat and back into your world. In yoga there is no hidden agenda, no place to impress. There is nowhere to go, no-one to be. Yoga gives us permission just to be… As we delve into the stretches and befriend our breath, we meet ourselves on the mat. Like greeting an old friend at the door, we embrace them, soften into their holding. We welcome their smiles, their tears, without judgement. We listen to them, empathise with them, enjoy all they are to us. We learn from them. Then they return to their world, their busyness, yet within us, we have captured something from the experience. We can't name it, yet it leaves its imprint on our soul, our spirit.

The Practice of Self Love

- ♥ For this pose come onto all fours.
- ♥ Stack your hands underneath your shoulders, shoulder-width distance apart and spread your fingers.
- ♥ Check your knees are underneath your hips and hip-width distance apart.
- ♥ Draw your belly towards your spine, feeling your spine is straight.
- ♥ Close your eyes and take a moment to find your breath. Observe your inhalations and exhalations.
- ♥ Eyes remaining closed, take a journey in your body. Feel your hands grounded on the earth and rising up the straws of your arms. Hollow out your armpits as if you are sucking them up towards the sky.
- ♥ Your heart is soft and open. Direct your breath towards the back of your heart and feel your heart expanding from the inside out; from front to back and side to side.

- ♥ Stay with your breath, as you roll your pelvis over your thighs, arching your spine and leading with your heart, as you draw your heart forward.
- ♥ As you exhale, drop your chin towards your chest rounding your spine up to the sky. Feel the base of your spine dip down towards your heels.
- ♥ Keep your eyes closed, gently moving through these two shapes as your body and breath dance together, letting the breath lead the way.
- ♥ After 5 or 6 breaths. Sit back on your heels and observe any changes in your relationship with your breath, mind and body.

For years I battled with my yoga practice, I wanted a fast, demanding practice which contorted my body into different shapes. I didn't listen or honour my body. It was a reflection of where I was in my life and where we were as a family. The pressure of life was entrapping us. Fed up with it all, we packed our bags and sold our beloved house, which held so many memories; we had only lived in it for four years, yet it had been filled with so many tears and was encapsulated with so much grief. And we left for Thailand. We released our burden of financial commitments to be free spirits. Looking back now, we ran away. We ran away from sorrow. Turning our backs to the life we knew, wanting to face something new. We hadn't the emotional strength to grow in the space we were currently in. Delving into my yoga I taught and practised for a least six hours a day. As I ached in my hips, stretched my hamstrings, opened my heart in backbends and contorted my body into different shapes, I thought my journey with yoga was there, I finally thought I understood the fascination with this ancient practice. However, yet again, I found myself pushing and stretching myself – not just on the mat but in life. I was mirroring myself again.

It was only when I was aged thirty-nine, unexpectedly pregnant and living in Asia, did I truly appreciate and understand the practice of yoga. Classed as an 'older women' and with a low-lying placenta I was advised not to do any exercise. Coming back from my hospital appointment, I unrolled my mat and cried. All my practice had given me over the past seven years was no longer available, or so I thought. It took all my resolve not to throw away my yoga mat. Instead I placed my hands on my belly and breathed. This was where my true practice began. The undoing, surrendering into the here and now, listening to my spirit.

Attunement

- ♥ Another pose that you can try for yourself is the child's pose. Kneel down, resting your bottom on your heels and bow forward rounding your spine so your head rests on or towards the mat. Extend your arms out in front.
- ♥ Stay here for a few moments feeling your breath rise through your body from the inside out. Take 5 breaths.
- ♥ On the next inhalation rise onto all fours. Move your knees slightly away from each other. Exhale here, then inhale and arch your spine, taking your gaze up skywards into cow pose. As you exhale bend your elbows, drop your chin and slide your body forward to lie on your belly. Inhale.
- ♥ Leading with your heart, lift your shoulders and upper chest off the floor; rising up into cobra. Exhaling, come back onto all fours then slide your bottom back onto your heels in child's pose. Stay for one breath. On your next inhalation lift up onto all fours and return to cow pose.
- ♥ Move with your breath. Exhale going down and inhale coming up into cobra. Exhale and return to child's pose. Repeat this flow. Move with your breath for 5 breaths, letting your breath lead you through the movements.
- ♥ Finally come into child's pose and rest there, feeling your breath. Observe any changes in your mind, body and spirit.

My yoga has been a journey, it has formed part of my journey and here I am now, back in the UK and a full-time working mother of three daughters. Daily I play a well-adjusted game of tug-of-war, some days it's juggling more balls than others and often many of them fall down or roll away. I am not very skilled yet I keep trying, goading myself that one day I will become proficient. As mothers there is no right or wrong way, each day presents itself differently for us to feel a path through it. Blindfolded.

We caress and nurture the soft parts, the ones which we can delve into without resistance. Yet, the areas we struggle with, that challenge us, are those we often fight against. We feel torn. How to feel more attuned? To feel balanced and grounded, settled and satisfied? How to find a place where we feel rooted and contented so we can flourish and blossom? A place we can extend from, reach out from with no feelings of restriction. As busy mothers we give so much and often feel torn. We push and pull ourselves in so many different directions that we rarely stop to take a breath.

Do we ever stop to enjoy the view, to fully appreciate a particular moment? How often we rush out of the door in the haze of the morning routine, running to school or work, but only when we come back home do we feel the peace, the tranquillity it offers? As we look at the piles of shoes near the front door and sigh in our hearts, we realise that in the madness of getting out, we missed something. Not missed something in terms of forgotten it, but missed *being*. Being with our children, being in the moment. It is only at times of stopping that we realise the quiet, the spaciousness and are able to enjoy the moment. Tenderly we put away the disarray of discarded clothes, tidy the beds, align the shoes, wash away the debris of breakfast mishaps, so we can enjoy the rest of the day. So we can delve into that space within the quietness, before the mayhem of children arriving again. Yoga is like that moment of coming home.

Refining the Art of Balance

- ♥ Give yourself time to centre and stand at the front of your mat with your feet outer hip-width distance apart. Look at your feet ensuring their outer edges are in line with the edges of your yoga mat. Lift your toes and spread them wide before placing them back down.
- ♥ Ground down through the ball of your big toe, little toe and inside, outside of the heel. Feel your feet firmly rooted to the earth.

- Take your weight over to the right, lifting your left foot onto your right foot. Then bring the sole of your left foot to the inside of your right shin, or right upper thigh. Ground down through your right foot whilst extending skywards through the crown of your head.
- Bring your hands to meet in prayer position in front of your heart. Find a place ahead to steady your gaze and breathe. Feel the presence of the pose; keeping your gaze steady. As you root down through your right foot, sense a drawing up of energy from the earth up your right leg, along your trunk and out through the crown of your head. Feel a sense of lightness as you balance.
- Be here in the moment. When we are balanced we are present. When we are present we feel balanced. Stay for 5 breaths.
- Come back to standing. Close your eyes and contrast your right leg with the left. Maybe your right leg feels heavier, more grounded, more connected? Notice where your awareness lies. When you feel ready repeat on your left leg.

Now this is your practice, transferring this sense of rootedness, connection, presence and balance into your life. Give yourself an invitation to be absorbed, to be totally immersed into the moment. Let the chaos of your life stand still, press the pause button. Notice, when you do, how at peace you feel in your world, how at peace you feel with the outer world. Even if it is just for a moment. Let that moment seep into your whole being, let it run through your veins. Soon that moment will become a nostalgic one, which will pass you by.

Let your practice be one of nurturing and nourishing yourself. Just like a tree needs the right conditions in order to blossom, in order to grow and flourish, so do we. We need to ensure we make time to nurture and nourish ourselves; to replenish our well, so we come from a place of feeling balanced, centred and rooted, so we have more to give as a mother, a partner, a daughter.

When we feel balanced, we feel the presence. When we are present we are embodied in the moment. The gift of being present secures our memories. Think of memories etched in your mind, when your emotions were raw: laughter, tears, sorrow. When the experience was so real and you were so immersed that you had no choice but to be absorbed into it. How often do we give ourselves fully to the moment, aside from childbirth and orgasms? When we truly listen to our inner calling, our innate wisdom and are so engrossed in the moment, that the outer world may be whirling around us, yet we feel rooted, stable, steady and at ease in ours.

The Warrioress

- Engage with your graceful power within as you take a wide stance along the length of your mat. Both feet facing forward.Turn your right foot 90° facing a short end of the mat. Check the heel of your right foot is in line with the inner arch of your left foot.
- Turn your hips away from your right leg towards your left foot. Hands on your hips.
- Stacking your trunk over the pelvis, inhale and extend your arms out to the side, shoulder height.
- Sense a tug-of-war action between your right and left arms, a pulling from your heart centre out through your finger tips, then draw the energy back into your heart centre.
- Bend your right knee so it stacks over the right ankle and your thigh is horizontal to the floor.
- Ground down through the outside edge of your left foot. Soften into your breath and breathe. Feel steady in the pose. Feel stable from your pelvis down to the ground and lightness from your core up towards your heart.
- This is the Warrior II – a pose which symbolises courage and stability. As you hold the pose for 5 breaths, set your intention. From this stable base, cultivate strength and courage to extend

outwards. Think about how you can use these gifts. Where in your life do you need courage to make changes, courage to settle into what is unfolding? Courage to be strong.

- ♥ When you are ready repeat Warrior II on the other side.

You are your own radiant goddess who has the capacity to shine, to illuminate paths for your children and let the essence of your being glow. Yoga helps captivate that brightness as you rewire your relationship with yourself, finding the truth and essence of who you are. We need to learn to release ourselves from the emotional taxes which innately attach to us as mothers. The guilt, the blame, the rock and roll pain which we carry in our hearts. Yoga helps us acknowledge, then feel, touch and experience the passing tides of all those emotions. As we sit with them and witness them as if they were clouds moving across the sky of our soul, only then can we to begin to honour ourselves through a seat of forgiveness, acceptance, faith, laughter, tears and love.

Let us do for ourselves what we do for our children. We love and praise them. We hold them, comfort them. We listen to their hearts. We love them.

Igniting Your Fire

- Take a comfortable sitting position, perhaps resting your back against something, as you will be here for a little while. Or choose to lie on your back. Take a few moments to read this, then close your eyes, meditate on the words and let them penetrate into your being. Feel them, touch them, and imagine them. Let them reverberate into your soul.
- Rest your hands on your belly and take a moment to feel your body. Acknowledge how it feels to be in your body: right here, right now, without thought or judgement.
- In your mind's eye, take a journey through your body, travelling from your toes, feet, along your legs. Feel your pelvis, spine, arms and hands. Be aware of areas which feel more open, parts of the body you feel more connected to. Parts which feel more closed, more tense.
- Be aware of those parts of your body which you are more familiar with, those you tend to avoid. Now embrace them all. Let your right side marry your left side, the bottom half with the top, the front of your body with the back. Welcome it all. Accept it all. Honour it all.
- Now feel your breath coming and going, as you grow aware of your belly and feel it rising and falling with the rhythm of your breath. As you draw your breath in, sense it rising from your

belly into your upper chest, to your heart centre. As you exhale, feel the breath recede from your upper chest and heart centre back down to your belly.

- Visualise yourself drinking in breath with your inhalation, as if you are filling a glass from the bottom, your belly to your heart centre – then pouring your breath out with your exhalation, from the top to the bottom.
- Stay here with your breath and mind. Keeping your left hand on your belly, bring your right hand onto your heart centre. Follow the path of your breath from belly to heart and from heart back down to the belly. In our belly resides our hara centre – our power, in our hearts – our love. Let your power flow to your heart and let your love flow to your power centre through your breath.
- Feel the power of love that resides within you. It flows in you, running through every single cell, through your entire being. See it as a golden light. Watch it travel to your toes, out to your fingers and through the crown of your head. Immerse yourself in this light. Feel the light's warmth radiating from the inside out, bursting out from every cell. Stay for a while bathing in this light. This is your light, own it, honour it, let it shine so brightly because YOU are that light. A radiant goddess. An amazing

woman. An amazing daughter, sister, lover, mother. See it, feel it, believe it. Be it.

Life is not always an easy journey, if it were you probably wouldn't be reading this. However, through your practice, whatever that is, yoga, meditation, life, you can offer yourself up for self-enquiry, to self-reflect and to grow. As we awaken to ourselves, we begin to listen. Witness our dreams, our aspirations, so we can find ways to live with them, live through them and live them out in our truth.

As a busy mother, life can seem relentless, frustrating and arduous as we find ourselves making compromises, sacrifices, as the roller coaster of life sweeps us along. We run on empty, have no time for a cuppa or a peaceful pee, let alone a yoga or meditation practice.

So, let our life be our practice not our practice be our life. So we can live our life authentically for the sake of our children and our children's children. It's just a passage of time.

Hindu mandala

Unexpected Gifts

Back to Laura

I RECENTLY CAME ACROSS A SOCIAL MEDIA IMAGE: a serene lake scattered lovingly with large paving stones popping out from the water and the caption underneath, so prominent it caught my mind's eye, 'Obstacles or Stepping Stones? You get to choose.' This resonated at such a level for me, as for the past four years I have chosen, and still choose now, to look at my life as one huge, empowered leap of faith, knowing that I am the *all power*. My determination, persistence and commitment to empower myself and others to expand with self-worth, to acknowledge myself as singer and songwriter, and have complete faith in life itself, inspire me to continue stepping intuitively and faithfully from one stone to the next. Sometimes, with a beautiful calm pool of water under me, I almost float from one stone onwards but other times, with a rough sea, high tide and torrential rain coming at me, I cling on and ride the waves… these are the times when I know I'm being given gifts, stepping stones for me to walk over and to embrace with determination and grace.

I would be deceiving you if I were to say that my path has been one of plain sailing, it's been very different from that. So often I've lost the compass, had to steer the ship against strong winds and keep going with only myself as captain, skipper, first mate, chef, passenger (not always first class!) and ship's officer. Obstacle or stepping stone? The choice is mine and mine alone and what always gives me strength is that I have the free will to look at and review my life, my beliefs, my dreams, my desires and to view perceived blocks either as heavy boulders that weigh me down, keeping me from my visions, or as inspired gifts that, once unwrapped, allow me to grow, expand, unfold and flourish as I love and accept myself even more and learn, learn, learn on my way. It's this choice that keeps me strong in mind, body and spirit and this choice brings me here, writing to you and uniting with these six determined women, each living in their truth and continuing through so-called adversity and achievements, with complete certainty – belief in themselves and in life. Through a deep inner knowing we create change for ourselves, our worlds and, along the way, inspire many, many others no different from us. We are not special and no more gifted than any person on this planet, we are simply determined to keep going through it all and to bring our messages to the world with love and confidence, opening our gifts every time sure that, whatever life brings, we are more than big enough to embrace or overcome.

You have the power
to unfold from your heart
and flourish with LOVE

What About Me?

Most of the time we stay busy trying to get through the day, fulfil everyone else's needs, get the job list done and focus on what we think needs doing to survive. It is only when we decide to PAUSE and take stock of what really matters, that we can continue *living* and *being* in our truth with real integrity towards our soul's path and purpose. It takes real courage, and devotion to having faith in our dreams, for this to come about, to pause for a while and put ourselves *first*, to 'live from the filled cup and let others have the overflow', as Iyanla Vantez puts it so perfectly. It can be a scary journey and yet the journey can also be a sacred one of complete soul fulfilment and excitement, as it allows for a deeper knowing of our own power and integrity, of what makes us tick, where we set our boundaries, how we put aside the *doing* and allow for *being;* what we are prepared to let go of so we can re-emerge to give space for the new. This is the journey of a brave Mama and I understand that, for many, this might feel out of reach; it seems easier, perhaps, to live a settled life in someone else's version of ourselves. However, I also know that, when the Mama is ready and the roar is brewing inside, nothing can stop her and the great thing is that the universe is always here saying YES!

Realising that we are more than enough unravels of what and who we are as spiritual and human beings, actually LIVING and BEING those qualities. In essence, as spiritual beings we are unconditional love and acceptance, kindness, compassion, bounteousness, receptivity, harmony, inner peace, forgiveness and patience. It is our birthright and work to live and be these qualities. This is what it means *to be*. Of course, growing up we each experience our own versions of others instilling their values in us and we can often carry these, together with our own collection of unhelpful messages, into adulthood where they subconsciously become a false knowing of our experiences. However we can release those messages and rewire the tracks through forgiveness and acts of self love. We can, very simply, create a NEW STORY, one that speaks of who we are *right now*, alongside what we are ready to become. We can express this and start to seed our desires in the now through the perspective we choose to live through. It's our choice and what a great legacy to impart to our children – one that teaches power, self love and devotion to living our dreams.

Throwbacks

Growing up I just loved singing and the feeling of exploring my voice in front of the mirror, of course with my hair brush, listening to Mary Hopkins, Abba, Barbara Streisand, Dusty. I loved, and still do love them. Hours watching musicals on TV and picturing myself as Ginger Rogers. Doing the steps, wearing the dresses, singing the songs – I loved the whole feel of how the voice could bring such power and emotion to life. I envisioned myself on that stage with the glamour, dresses, hair, make-up and singing my song. I rehearsed musicals in the privacy of my room, seeing myself singing the parts even though inside I didn't quite believe this could ever be me and felt that my voice should be kept quiet. I was always conscious of not wanting to be heard, never felt good enough or that I could possibly be my own star, on stage doing my thing. It was one big fantasy that I never believed could be for me.

Being told to leave the school choir at thirteen, as I was 'out of tune with the rest of the singers', didn't do much for my singing esteem either, so I stopped singing, believing or even dreaming that I could ever go on a stage and sing my song. My self-esteem and self-belief became generally weak and this showed up in so many ways in my life as I often failed to get up and keep going. I was interpreting messages from my peers and teachers, and of course myself, that I wasn't good enough and just accepted this as who I was. Throughout my teens and onwards, I attracted experiences that verified my feelings of low self-worth, bringing unfulfilling relationships, financial uncertainty, meaningless work, living my life through the lens and expectation of others, unaware that I could feel great simply being ME. Today, I know these experiences were my schoolroom for growth and for this I am so grateful.

Spirit and truth always shine through and from an early age and into my teens, I had a great need to fulfil my deeper life questions. Born into a Jewish family, the only things that really sat well with me about that were the humour and the food, especially my Nana's chopped liver! As for the rest of it, well religion just didn't click in with my beliefs and unanswered questions. Being told that God was in a building more than in me didn't make sense at all, especially as I was only expected to visit that building twice a year! I was on a different quest, a less religious but more spirituall journey. In my twenties and thirties, stuck in an unhelpful pattern of work, money, low self love and acceptance, I was on a trail of lack-lustre living, following the thoughts of those I allowed to influence my life, always in fear of making great change and generally going through the motions of other people's dreams that I adopted as my beliefs. Singing was still very much on the back burner. In my twenties, I chose to look more deeply by turning to spiritual classes and texts where I opened my mind to teachers and authors that resonated with what I believed as spiritual truth – I released the need for structured religion in my life. Looking within, I turned to meditation and loved it, and so began my journey of seeking answers to those questions I felt were so important. This was a beautiful first encounter with the world within me and one that I always treasure in my heart.

The one important ingredient I was unaware of then, but I realise now, is that we are each, in every moment, consciously and unconsciously creating our lives. What's more, the bits we don't like and would rather ignore or brush under the carpet – yes, aren't we great at that? – are here as huge parts of our healing, learning and transformation, to be used as big learning tools; gifts for empowered growth. To create lasting change it takes readiness to embrace a whole new way of being and complete willingness to take full responsibility for all we are – to LOVE all that we are and, in doing so, learn empowered ways to look within, forgive the old and embrace the new.

This knowing took many years to realise and faithfully embrace as part of my life so, as I embody this way of living more and more each day, I pray that you can follow my words here to embed new principles in your heart, consciousness and mind, allowing you to tune in effortlessly to your own power; to live your fullest and most expressed life possible.

BREATHE

in

LOVE

She Made it Here

Fifteen years ago, as I was preparing to bring my treasured daughter into this life, there were many situations around me that I felt were out of my control. I perceived them as happening *to* me and I still had a poor understanding of myself being the co-creator of my life. Breaking away from my daughter's father before she was born and facing life as a new mum, I was just about getting through each day as I picked up the pieces of my situation and just got on with it. With a screaming baby and post-natal blues, my life felt completely outside my control; but how wrong I was! I just didn't get it.

It was ten years later, in 2012 with another failed relationship gone by, that I was bought to my knees, to a place of complete surrender but guided to complete the *You Can Heal Your Life* coach training in San Diego. Here on a Sacred Labyrinth walk, my real awakening took place. The labyrinth, a walkable spiral pattern created on the ground, can be a glorious tool for contemplation as it allows for silence and deep reflection. During my walk, the deeper life questions that I had pushed away and ignored for so many years, just surfaced and I finally *got it*. There, I realised my reason, my truth, my calling in life and WOW..! what an immense experience of awakening that was, to know that my life really is held in my own hands. Years of seeking outside myself stopped right there. I was called to take complete responsibility for my whole life. No more blame, no more resentment, no more running, no more ignoring my part in it all; I was profoundly called to justice, through the path of the Sacred Labyrinth. My journey on my path of self-knowledge was about to begin as I was summonsed to the only place that truly exists – *within*.

In that moment I received the answers to many questions; and from then I have only needed to look deep within me, where I now know the mystery lies. The most empowered understanding is that I don't need to do much to experience the fullness of my life, because the *doing* is in the *being*, and the more I allow myself to know my worth, to know what makes me feel good, to honour what I am here for, to love and accept myself unconditionally, to live in my gifts and consciously create life in the way I desire, then life simply and miraculously brings me exactly what I need to experience and live fully… as if by magic

Coming home from my newfound knowings, I was inspired to discover more of myself spiritually and have, since then, devoted myself as a student of truth. Yes! My voice surfaced and my hairbrush days were ready to reclaim themselves, this time out of the closet! I'm so so grateful for my openness to trust those steps into the unknown and for allowing my true singing voice and words of love to connect with each other, as I embarked on my calling: to sing my songs and bring them to life.

Amazingly, I did this not by striving to create my life as a singer, nor *making* it happen. It was a simple act of following my heart in faith, doing what I love doing and allowing life to lead me on a golden path that has opened up a world of magic and possibilities. Yes, of course I took inspired action, which is vital, but not with steps of fear or uncertainty, they were steps of loving faith in what I believe.

The steps included writing down the seventeen meditations that had emerged from my labyrinth walk, being guided to guitar lessons, literally bumping into songstress and voice coach Kate Daisy Grant on a Sunday walk and being guided to Jason my partner in life, love and music. Before we even met, he had already written music which perfectly fitted my lyrics to *Do You Know*, a song I had written six months earlier! I go on composing songs and music with Jason, continuing our mission to birth our songs. And life flows on and on, as I'm blessed with more songs, and writing *Mama on a Mission* to help empower you to live your dreams too… All this happened for me because I was ready. Ready to surrender to *me*, to learn more, to *be* more, to give more, ready to let go of the old, to live in faith, and ready to embrace what I love doing. This can't be taught from outside ourselves without readiness, nor learned from self-help books in the local book store on a Saturday afternoon, although it may seed from there. It's a journey of allowing life in, even through pain, and the point of no return is when we discover what really makes us tick and want to leap out of bed every morning for it. It's sometimes scary, always unexpected but never boring.

These days, I create songs to inspire inner transformation and empower the soul, in which the messages and positive affirmations can be used as tools for changing thoughts and beliefs. Listened to daily, over and over, songs on *The Gift, Now* and *Metamorphosis* albums are loving guides to releasing the old and embracing the new. I consciously state intentions and desires for my life, along with practising visualisation, intuitive visioning and seeking, through prayer, specific details and clarity about the feeling and experience that I want. Practicing forgiveness, gratitude, journalling and unconditional loving kindness to myself, and so arriving at complete conviction and belief, these are the rich tapestry of empowered tools and techniques that I use daily as I embrace the *now* and live a fully-expressed life of love, abundance and joy. My daily spiritual ritual is as vital as breathing, as it grounds and strengthens me allowing space for deep inner belief, especially through times of uncertainty.

The power of these techniques go way beyond explanation in the space of this book and I lovingly teach them in my private consultation practice. So, in these pages, I share with you a few practices that have empowered my life, and might inspire you to walk with your imagination through the gateway of self-creative expression. They include visioning, faith and forgiveness and can empower you to live in the freedom you deserve.

The past four years have been a constant reminder of how astounding life really is and how, when we know the power of our selves, and embrace faith, belief, power, forgiveness, self love, intuitive focus and inspired action with complete commitment, we can be vessels for aligning with and receiving miracles in life. This is an art, yet we are each and every one of us capable of using this power to create our dream reality. For me there is one choice, I either fester in the old or *unfold* in the new – I choose to unfold. We are only really ever working with our thoughts, beliefs and that invisible energy we call life, but mastering them is a journey of pure patience as well as openness to a lifetime of learning that offers a pot of gold to those brave, bold and willing artists who are ready to freely and imaginatively create beauty on life's unlimited blank canvas.

In 2012 I had no conscious idea that I would, by now, have created three albums of songs with more on their way, written a book and be inspiring people to know their worth. Of course, there are times of uncertainty, fear, financial blips and, dare I say it, self-doubt? Even so, when I return to the changeless and loving place within me and connect with my truth, I am shown the way again and again; with a constant willingness to surrender, listen and love myself, I am so very blessed.

Up to date. And here I am doing what I love, amazed at how my life has evolved such a short time. I'm through the other side of two heart-wrenching relationships, brought in my ultra adventurous daughter on her solo journey and continue connecting the dots on my way to being the best mum that I can be. I've met Jason, written and created beautiful albums, evolved as student and teacher of metaphysics on a life long path and continue to introduce self love, abundance-awareness and consciousness to those who cross my path. I still live with the vulnerability of creating a business and remaining in my truth, but feel the deepest faith that I am being rightly guided on my way. And I can assure you that my faith in *me* has been tested rigorously.

Visioning

You may know clearly what your highest vision is for life and why you are here. If so, you have a definite springboard into your desires and dreams. But frequently, we have blocks, knowing there is more to life yet we can't grasp it, see it, live, feel or even believe it, and this leaves us blurry and uncertain. This is not at all helpful, I've been there and still experience uncertainty, especially when I look back to the void of the first forty-odd years of my life. It wasn't a great place to be, but I am eternally grateful for it because, wrapped inside that empty feeling, were so many gifts that led to eventual transformation.

Each and every one of us is here now to fulfil our lives and desires, and that doesn't mean changing the world, although that would be a great reason to be here! More simply, it means living in complete knowing satisfaction that we are following our hearts' desires, living fulfilled, fully-expressed lives and loving every moment as we become more aware of ourselves.

Realising what we want means putting ourselves first, regardless of what we imagine others might think or feel, it means devoting time to *you* and really listening to your inner wisdom; that's what I mean by living life fully expressed – it's our birthright. Reaching this place means surrendering all shame and guilt, a trait that we women love to carry, and choosing to let go of fear as we discover and set our intentions for life. The universe, which moves mountains to bring our desires, is ready and waiting for you to get it together. But we can only receive from life when we are clear about what we want and have faith that it's possible.

So, what makes *your* heart sing? What gets you leaping up with joy in the morning? What are you overly excited about for your life? These are what you must acknowledge and allow yourself to be clear on. Take some time out, be silent and *ask* what you are called here for now. You really will receive answers and these answers are your truth, no-one else's truth, your truth and that's what you are here for, to *live fully* in your truth, free of guilt or shame or fear and loving each moment. GIVE YOURSELF PERMISSION TO SHINE. This book is an enabling tool for you to live your personal truth and the first step to setting off this new spiral of motion right now is for you to learn to connect with the highest visions and callings for your life and bring them to the forefront of your conscious imagination – let life bring them to life.

We so often focus intently on what we *don't* want that all we seem to attract is *more* of what we don't want; how does that work? Well, the universe responds to our predominant thoughts, so if we spend 80% of the time focusing on the unwanted then that's what we'll attract. The subconscious memory stores 95% of our thoughts and beliefs, tucked away where we're not even aware of those old messages, yet through a process I call *intuitive visioning*, you can easily access stored thoughts and messages and bring them into the light, ready to be changed by supportive, positive statements, declarations and affirmations. We have a tendency to listen to what we *think* is the inner voice of intuition and wisdom but that's can be our ego voice telling us what we want to hear and we are not always listening to our truth, so try using the art of deep listening.

Visioning Questions

Give yourself quiet time to ask yourself these questions, look within and *feel* the answers that come up. Visioning is a profound process, very different to visualisation. I use visioning most days and find it so valuable as it allows me to connect deeply with my own knowing. It is my beautiful friend, the source of intuition, a higher intelligence that connects with Spirit's voice and speaks when we are in stillness. Visioning is a great ritual to embrace and play with. It calls for silence, space and time to go within and befriend the knowing that is always there, ready with your answers. You are the only person who knows your own truth. No-one can tell you what it is, how it should be, or how to go about following your path. Believe me. I made my life around others for so long and it just doesn't work. The individual will that we each possess is our gift and it's up to us to honour and cherish all the messages coming to us, because they guide us through life to our desires, dreams and highest visions.

Take a moment here and ask yourself in silence –

♥ What AM I here for and I called to give to life?

♥ What do I have to offer this life NOW?

♥ What can I let go of now to clear the way for my good?

♥ What can I embrace more of now?

♥ What else could I know for my Highest Good to keep me on my true path?

The Visioning Process

- In silence and alone give yourself space and some time to connect within.
- Have your journal and pen ready.
- Look at your first question.
- Close your eyes for three minutes and connect within by focusing on your heart space and feeling the LOVE that's always there.
- Ask the question three times and simply allow the answer or messages to come – it may take time and may not be obvious but your openness and willingness to continue will allow you to tap into a deep inner communication that is waiting for you – be patient.
- Now open your eyes and write the answer in your journal – free of judgement.
- You are being told your truth – simply allow it and let the answers flow.
- Give thanks and continue to the next question patiently allowing the answers to arise. Repeat this exercise and journal daily for two weeks, building to a month and you'll be amazed at the messages and wisdom that arise.

Visioning is a meditational tool that takes us from the silence within to a place of deeper listening, beyond chatter and expected thoughts, opening up insight to show what is here for us. Visioning opens us to truth, we may not always like or even understand the answers we receive, however, it is truth and as we place our limited thoughts and beliefs aside for a while and simply surrender in the silence, we can be surprised at the clarity that appears, where we are guided and what inspired action we are guided towards. Meditation, after all, is a spiritual tool for us to deeply connect with Source, where all the answers lie within us. Intuitive visioning allows us to get in touch with our gut feeling or deeper inner knowing. It's a wonderful guidance system readily available and waiting for you to use, today. It only needs you to plug in and turn on, though by ignoring its call we would be ignoring our higher self wanting to guide us to our highest vision.

Messages that arise may not always be tangible action steps to take. Many a time I am guided to speaking to a certain person, connecting with a work partner or taking time out for myself. Watch out for them because these messages can often present in extremely subtle whispers about *ways of being* such as allowing in more love, letting go of control, feeling the fear and going ahead regardless... and these, for me, are the golden nuggets, the true enlightened gems that shift me from one place in my thinking directly to the truth. Daily intuitive visioning is what guides me on and empowers me to live my dreams and desires.

You may not always like what you hear! Often we ignore the truth, run, hide, zone out, have another glass of wine, in my case cuppa tea! Sometimes we lie to ourselves or, at the other extreme, live a full on life of pretence, to side step the truth. But there is no hiding and we know that when we run we take ourselves with us; eventually, in one way or another, the truth arises and can show up in ways we don't feel great about. This is when it matters most to listen, surrender and just allow those messages to come, acknowledging there is work to be done. The most wonderful thing is, whatever we are going through, however bad it seems, the pain is a messenger and there is a way through it – we can begin in any moment to look within and connect to our deeper knowing. This is where the magic begins. Go slowly and lovingly with yourself, knowing you are always safely guided; acknowledge that you are doing your best and are ready to be compassionate, kind and patient in the course of living your life from the inside out. Start from where you are in the *here and now.*

Now, I am not suggesting that to find your life's purpose you have to hop on a plane, travel to the US, as I did, and submerge yourself in seven days of silent retreat and self-discovery to get to the heart of your blocks, beliefs, dreams and desires, however enticing this idea might be! I know that you can begin right here and now, wherever you are, just as you are, with whatever is going on around you; you can take the first steps to loving and accepting yourself unconditionally and begin the empowered journey of living your life in your way. You can take time to be in stillness and silence with a simple walk in nature, connecting to life and going within for a while to ask what it is that you are here to be. The healing songs from the albums *Now*, *The Gift* and *Metamorphosis* are guidance for looking more deeply at loving yourself and revealing your life purpose; for transforming your thoughts and feelings and reaching a connected place of self love and acceptance.

There is always a certain way to connect back to yourself.

Butterfly mandala

www.Millande.com

From Disaster to Divinity

Patricia Iris Kerins

DEAREST READER,

I AM DELIGHTED TO HAVE BEEN INVITED to share some of my life's journey here with you in an effort to help YOU become more of YOU. I will start at the beginning, as they say, a very good place to start! I will give you a taste of what it was like to be me all those years ago and how I have addressed the issues that emerged. It is incomplete as it would be a whole book on its own; I do give you some juicy bits though.

1950s

I was born in the '50s; I know that things have improved a lot since then – or have they? They have in my world because I have steadily worked through my stuff and become incredibly clear.

1993

It wasn't until I was flying up the road to Inverness from Birmingham in 1993 at the age of forty-three, almost as if my car had wings, that I realised I was loveable. Yes, that's right – I discovered, having attended an amazing one-week, Louise L. Hay workshop entitled *Love Yourself, Heal Your Life*, that I was indeed loveable and that it's okay to love yourself.

This was news to me because until that point I had been desperately trying to fit in, to be someone that others would find acceptable, anyone, in fact, other than being my true authentic self because *she*, according to them out there, simply wasn't good enough!

Family Background

I had been brought up in a very critical and judgemental family energy with strict disciplines in place. The end result of living with that was I truly felt not good enough at anything, not seen or heard and my opinion was not sought; indeed it didn't matter. I was insignificant; *I* didn't matter.

The result was I grew up into a tall, shy girl with rounded shoulders as I tried to play small and disappear, BUT – and it's a big but – with a revolutionary rebel bubbling away inside me. I was blessed with the big gift of a good singing voice, so there was the duality. I was encouraged to sing at competitions and concerts but told to 'shut up' at home, not only by my parents but particularly by my siblings. I felt truly rejected as when I did get up and sing as required, my brothers accused me of showing off. So, that is the way it was – damned if you do, damned if you don't! These days, I would know that was emotional abuse at some level.

Mother's Advice

My mother's advice was a pure survival strategy along the lines of 'let them (the men folk) think they have the answers', 'make it look as if it were their idea'. I was told that men didn't like smart-mouthed women, to put my gas on a peep! Equally, I was assured I didn't need to say anything at all; the look on my face said everything – a no-win situation once again!

I really began to feel inadequate, and yet there was a fire in me that knew this was not the way life was meant to be, and I would steadfastly refuse to go to the fridge to get beers for my brother. I always was very cheeky (in their terms), just saying, 'What did your last servant die of? I didn't come here to serve you!' We fought a lot.

Darkness

I also felt I had come in with a darkness around me. I was depressed often and didn't laugh very much. I observed others acting that way, but I really didn't want to be like that. Little did I know then, as I do now, that I came in and on to this planet with a lot of luggage from past lives and ancestral programming; it was in my bones and my genes!

My ancestors had weighed me down with their old paradigms of negative, limiting beliefs, added to the suppression of feminine energy that has gone on for millennia. This still affects all women at a cellular level. Most are completely unaware of that, and yet our whole world shows us how women are regarded as second to men. Females are to be kept down and under control. It is a measure of how powerful we are that they feel they need to control and manipulate us at every turn when all we need and desire is to be regarded as equal; yet we are acknowledged as different in every way. The males are not going to do that until we truly see and respect ourselves and demonstrate how powerful and complete we are. It all starts with us.

Ah! The benefit of hindsight – here was I, a teenager in the '60s coping with I knew not what; however, the music of Mendelsohn's *Violin Concerto* and Beethoven's *Moonlight Sonata* eased the pain. Music was always my place of solace and comfort. My parents were both professional musicians, and I was born and brought up in a world of music, thank goodness. That world also included Cliff and the Beatles, the Kinks and the Rolling Stones.

Drink

I remember that, when I started going out with guys to parties in my late teens, I would take a drink before going out to steel my nerves. Self-conscious I was in every respect, with no self-confidence or self-esteem. Drinking allowed me to let go of my inhibitions, and I could become the party animal that I thought everyone found acceptable. I became that totally fun, over-the-top woman that everyone wanted to know, and I became popular even as I lost many days to massive headaches and sickness due to the alcohol.

I met my first husband when I was sixteen, and we were married when I was nineteen, playing straight into the paradigm of getting married and having two children when young. It didn't last as it was based on a fantasised romantic love which, in reality as I look back, was very romantic but had no real substance. However, I learned a lot, and no children had come along.

Spiritual Searching

As far back as I can remember, I was searching for Jesus. It had to be Jesus, and I went to every place of worship in Glasgow where I was born, including tabernacles, chapels, and churches. I listened intently to everything ministers had to say; I sang in choirs all over the city. Still, I didn't find the Jesus

I knew and loved. I had clearly come on to the planet knowing him very well, so that search was always in vain.

Religion

Religion, it seemed to me, was a sorry thing of rules, regulations, and dogma – not a lot of LOVE present; no compassion or forgiveness. So I gave it up. It was not fulfilling in any way at all, except for the singing in the choirs.

I held my spiritual connection in my heart until my sacred journey and obsessive spiritual drive began to take a deep hold of me; that wasn't until the age of thirty-three, a significant age, when my father died. I realised at that point that we are all here for a finite time, and the party girl had to go. I had to show up and do what I had come on the planet to do and be, or at least investigate that. There had to be more to life than what was currently on the menu! I was working non-stop and out singing semi-professionally in the evenings. Life was hectic with no quality, and time with my father had gone. I had been Daddy's girl, and now he was no longer there to accompany me at concerts.

It was time to live my life more consciously, not living aimlessly, understanding we are here for a purpose; for me, that purpose was around love, compassion, and forgiveness, and it had to start with me.

Self-punishment

I had really made a lot of mistakes, or so I self-judged. After my first marriage ended, I slept around with too many men who couldn't give a damn about me. For seven years I was in my masculine energy, playing the game of *love 'em and leave 'em* more effectively than the guys did. It became a kind of self-punishment for having been the one to break up my marriage that should, on paper, have worked. My self-esteem was rock-bottom, and the feeling of not being good enough was camouflaged by alcohol-fuelled bravado.

Relationships

Having said all of the above, I realised that relationships were going to be key to my taking control of my life in some measure, and the *first, last, and most important relationship I had in my life* was the one I was having with me.

My goodness, what a revelation that was, as I drew all my awareness back within! That is what took me to that Louise Hay workshop in the first instance as I started on a course to live a conscious life of self love. This meant loving myself in every way, with every fault, with the chequered past, with (society would tell me) the not perfect attributes of figure or height or boob size or any of these things. How inadequate was I? I had been telling myself that for so long! Now I was choosing to have a real look at how I spoke to myself, noting the abysmal effect it had on me.

The truth was that I would berate the parts of my body that didn't come up to the ten-out-of-ten mark. I would compare myself to others and put myself down. I would generally do a number on myself, sabotaging my efforts. A lot of the time, criticising others made me feel better; it more than took the pain away. My self-worth was zero, my self-esteem not much better, and I suddenly realised I was my own worst enemy. I didn't need any other enemies; I did it for me. I shot myself in the foot every single time!

A New Day Dawned

This is the good bit; this is the bit in my section of this book where I can say to you categorically that, by learning a new way of relating to myself, I have developed a love for my life. I AM the love in my life, and I grow LOVE MAGIC and LOVE POWER in my life by doing some of the simplest things every day. I have dedicated my life to becoming and being all I can be.

By doing that I have been able to reach out to thousands over the years and help them do exactly the same. It doesn't matter where you are starting from; you could be, like I was, fairly well down the pan or just halfway down the pan. You can get your climbing boots on and begin to CLIMB OUT OF THE PAN because if I can do it anyone can. I don't have any doubts about that!

Okay, let's go!

Your Voice

Your voice is amazingly powerful, whether you choose to use it by speaking, chatting, singing, sounding, writing or indeed in any way you can think of. It is a singular and yet whole expression of who and what you are, so be clear about that.

There are, at the time of writing, about 7.5 billion people on the planet, and there is ONLY ONE OF YOU! Yes, that's right, so, whatever your beautiful name is, they broke the mould when they made you. No one else has your eye print, fingerprint, heart print, or brain wave print, and no one has your DNA. It is not even certain that an identical twin would duplicate that, although I believe it has happened.

Have you received this message? Feel into it... no one else on the planet is in any way like you, so you are incomparable. Competition is not possible as you cannot compete on a level playing field, no two people being the same.

Wow, just think of the magnificent strand of life that you are, with all your unique gifts and talents that weave into and amongst this gorgeous, rich tapestry that is awaiting your singular signature, soul sound, tune, book, artwork, love, child, light, laughter – well I could go on forever. What a list! You are awesome! You are unique and not just because I say so – it is a fact!

Your First Solo

- So you can start using that fab voice of yours by saying first of all quietly into yourself, in a nice quiet place where you will not be disturbed:

I Am Unique

- Gently bring that outside and begin to get louder and louder, then start adding some colour and tone:

I Am Unique
And I Am Lovable
Just As I Am

- Woo hoo! Now build up the decibels. There's MORE! Here we go; we are on a roll.

- Whatever follows the two words 'I Am' in your inner dialogue defines who you are and how you are feeling. If you are feeling down (I Am depressed, anxious, tired, fed up), then CHOOSE to RAISE your vibes. Lift your spirits with this amazing self-talk mantra.

- Say or shout it out loud at least twenty times and make it your daily mantra:

I Am Good Enough

I Am Enough

I Am

If you are doing this in the car folk may think you've lost the plot, and hey, you have – CELBRATE LOSING THE OLD PLOT! You are stepping out of the well-worn path to purgatory, taking your power back from all those who have tried to tell you any different all your life.

Even though…

Here are another two words that are amazingly powerful. They can start wonderful sentences that acknowledge who and what you are doing and being right now and put you immediately into a state of transition as they imply a change. Certainly, there is one on the way. When you feel anxious, for example, start by acknowledging it, with:

Even though I am feeling anxious…

Then slot in the change and shift to a higher place:

I am choosing right now to let it go with love.

Why?

Because I really love myself and I know I am doing my best at all times.

Okay, now look at that all together in one sentence:

Even though I AM feeling anxious, I am choosing right now to let it all go with love and forgiveness because I really love myself, and I know I am doing my best at all times.

You may think that it's all very well to be saying that, but it doesn't feel true; *I don't love myself!* You are absolutely right; it is not all going to change immediately just by saying a few positive statements. You, like me, are a work in progress. Learning to love yourself fully and completely needs constant attention, so you could choose to change the phrase to the following example:

Because I am learning to truly love myself…

Affirmations like this really work because you are reprogramming your subconscious mind. It doesn't know what is true and what isn't – it accepts what you are saying as the way it is, so be mindful when you go off on a negative, self-inflicted diatribe of judgement. If you say these *positive* affirmations hundreds of times a day, you will replace the old programme in your mind with new ones. Believe me, it works!

We really are very sophisticated computers, and we need to choose to overwrite old programmes and replace them with brand new positive ones. A great one to try, and so simple, is just to say the one word *YES* for three minutes. Yes! Just keep saying it over and over and notice how you feel afterwards. You will have to push through a hiatus round about the two-minute mark; that is when the energy shifts. You will be giggling and laughing; your vibrations will be so high, and all because you are charging your energy up with positivity – it works!

Ego and Resistance

When we first start to truly love every aspect of ourselves, warts and all, it can feel odd and resistance can come up. We feel reluctant to do the exercises we need to do for change. It is fear coming from your ego. You see, your ego has kept you pretty much under control for many years as it looked outwards at all times, allowing the outside world to dictate how your life would be, and you danced to that tune.

Now you are taking your power back from your ego, and the outside world doesn't overly like that. It will tell you that this is daft, it won't work, and lots more unprintable stuff!

Write Your Letter

You just have to love your ego. If you listened to it day after day, you'd never have the confidence to do anything! So, take a deep breath and write a letter to your ego. Simply say:

> *Dear Ego,*
>
> *I love you; however, I am now taking all my power back from you. I am in charge. My heart is the leader here, and as I learn to go within and talk to my heart, I know it will take me to all the right situations, relationships and opportunities in my life. Thank you for everything you have done; now it is my time, my heart's time, and I call all my power back from you.*

You can do that by going within to visualise that very exercise. It is such a powerful thing to do, and this is you self-empowering, healing and loving yourself!

Creating Your Sacred Space

To centre yourself and prepare for a deeper meditation I am going to ask you to take *sacred space*. Now, what is that? I hear you ask. Well, it is simply this:

- Go to your favourite room, place in the garden, hut, conservatory, or wherever it is where you can sit down comfortably and KNOW you will not be disturbed for half an hour to an hour.
- Put up a DO NOT DISTURB, I AM MEDITATING sign and explain what you are doing.
- Next, clear the space by lighting a candle, and as the flame ignites, intend with your inner willpower that this room is cleansed of all negative energies. (There are more ways of clearing rooms on my youtube channel, demonstrating exactly this.)
- Then dedicate the space to hold your energy energetically in your highest vibration. Brilliant, well done!
- Now, sit down, cover yourself with a blanket if you wish, close your eyes and *RELAX*. Breathing deeply and rhythmically for a few breaths, deeper out than in, helps to truly relax you.

Visualisation

That brings us nicely to visualisation. As in meditation, where we close our eyes and allow ourselves to sink deep inside to relax and unwind, we go into our own inner landscape. With visualisation, we go further by employing our powers of imagination and the third eye. We have three eyes, two that look to the outer world and a third at the centre of the brow that looks within. It gathers your intuition, inner knowing and insights, seeing all that is going on at a deeper level.

I love to live in this world. My world within is so wonderfully pleasant and exciting and is the seat of my creative inspiration, because this is where I can talk with anyone I want at any time - fancy a blether with Oprah Winfrey? Nicole Kidman? Why not? - you can do it all on this level. You can create your own inner movie or play and anything you choose to do or be. You become your own film director, playwrite or composer; the inner world is your oyster.

If someone is guiding you through an exercise then follow and allow yourself to go with it. Some people see colours and not things, that is okay. Some see everything in detail, that is okay, some see bits and pieces or just get the feeling of it, that too is okay. We all have different ways of experiencing our inner world. To practice visualising, close your eyes and imagine yourself in the kitchen. See yourself at the sink. What is on your right, on your left and straight ahead? Open the cupboards go in and when you have done there, go into the lounge. You will be astounded as to how accurate your inner sight is. Happy visualising!!!

Your Turn to Visualise

Read through this practice once or twice and then close your eyes to visualise. Your beautiful eyes are powered by your brain and mind which are so sophisticated they have recorded every aspect of your life in full HD colour, and you can instantly recall it all. Try this one out:

- ♥ See yourself as you walked into your favourite supermarket last time – what you bought, who you spoke to, how much you paid. Focus on the detail. Great work! Well done. Now you are ready to create on a visual level.
- ♥ As you breathe slowly and peacefully, allow yourself to sink deeper and deeper, right down into your heart space. Just know, with a sense of awe, that you are accessing your heart in

a totally new and different way. Feel the beat of your heart and listen to it as it pumps blood around your body. That is the physicality of your heart. You might like to picture it as it pumps the blood. See the blood going smoothly, happily, on its way. As you focus on that, feel yourself becoming calmer and calmer; you might even want to repeat to yourself the words *relax, peace, calm.*

♥ Your emotional heart, for it has an energetic body too, may be feeling a little scared. This is new, so there may be a frisson of nerves, as you take the first conscious step to allowing your heart to lead your life.

When you were just a foetus in your mother's womb, blood started to circulate through your unformed body, and then your little heart began to beat; after that, your brain began to form, so you know that blood is your prime nourisher and the heart has always been your leader. It is just society that would have you believe it is your frenetically busy mind that is important. I call my heart my squadron leader, as when I truly listen to its every nuance, I know I fly high, very high!

Invocations

I feel it is always a wonderful way into any spiritual exercise to 'call in' the beautiful Angelic and Illumined Beings that you would like to be with you, as you work. It is different for everyone, as some may like to call forward the Fairy Kingdoms, the Archangels, the Ascended Masters or Star Beings – whatever it is for you. Think about who you resonate with and then try something like this. Once you get used to it you can use your own words, however the "most high" bit is important so that you get the highest vibrational presence possible.

Your Sacred Invocation

I invite you to read this through before beginning the invocation. Then, in silence, close your eyes and open your heart to the words and feelings.

Choose to call in your own guides and angels to work with. If this is a new concept to you, please *trust* that your guardian angel, is always there with you; ask for signs. When I first did this, I was inundated with signals they were around –

anything from white feathers flowing down in front of me to noticing car numbers like 111 or 333, which are very auspicious in a numerological way. Or perhaps coins will appear in your path or books that you need to read will fall off the shelf into your hands. When you *ask* your guides and angels to be with you, you will undoubtedly be aware of their presence. Give it a try; ask them in, right now, to be with you during your visualisation today and always. Say quietly inside, *I now invoke my beautiful Angels of Love and Light to be with me as I visualise and work with my heart energy.*

Here is a gentle visualisation for you to start your practice.

Connecting with your Guardian Angel

- Take sacred space, in other words go to a place or room where you can be in peace and quiet with a guarantee of no disturbance for at least 30 minutes.
- Close your eyes and focus on your breathing. Trace the breath IN and the breath OUT, allow it to deepen and allow yourself to relax more and more.

- On every OUT breath, affirm silently, *I am allowing myself to relax more and more, I am relaxed now.*
- As you do this you will find yourself sinking deeper and deeper within yourself, your beautiful being which is full of loving light.
- Take a journey around your body with your awareness, to breathe into each part. Breathe into your left foot, ask it to relax then your right foot, ask it to relax and then onwards using the same procedure with the right hand, left hand, left shoulder, right shoulder, right buttock, left buttock and so on. Allow each beautiful piece of you to relax and thank them for the wonderful service they perform for you every single day on the planet.
- Take your focus into your eyes now, first the right and then the left, then the nose, the mouth and tongue. You are allowing relaxation to spread through your body like a gorgeous elixir of liquid love.
- Now fill and flood every muscle full of love, then flood every major organ; take your time. You are feeling deliciously heavy and relaxed.
- This is a good time to go on a little journey. If you would like to meet your guardian angel, simply call her forward now. Hear yourself, in your own head, calling your beautiful guardian angel to come into your heart centre where you can

see or hear her, or perhaps just feel her presence. There she is, that's right, you are not seeing or hearing things she is reaching out to you, answering your call.

- What is her or his name, how about asking? Do that now and LISTEN for the answer.
- Does she have a message for you today? Ask and you will receive one.
- When you come back to the room, take time to write down everything in your journal, as it will be great to look back and plot your growth with this new way of being.
- When you are ready *gently* bring yourself back into your body, into the awareness of your breath and send beautiful roots down into the ground. Increase your breathing and when you feel ready, open your eyes. Look around. Your world will seem sharper and sparkly!

Well done. Get writing now and drink lots of water.

Forgiveness

Some people say that they are not ready to forgive or they could never forgive the actions of the other person. When this happens, you block yourself from ever healing. The offenders are not aware of that; the only one that continues to suffer from this is YOU.

We can compromise a little here. If you say *I am willing to forgive you*, the Universe hears and will put the forgiveness into motion. You see, love is FORGIVING; when you can love at a high level, all heals. You feel better and the other is released. You now let them go, giving great thanks for their input in your life, for the lesson, for the opportunity that your soul has had to grow in love from that whole scenario. It may have been extremely tough; however, my experience is that the Goddess never gives you more to deal with than you can handle.

For your continued support and healing, I have recorded an MP3 with particular healing protocols, so if you visit my website www.patriciairiskerins.com and go to the shop, you will see it there, where you can download it free of charge. It is always very powerful to have someone guide you on your journey, and yet you can still make it your own.

This powerful healing protocol has transformational effects; when you do it, say, three times a week for a few weeks, it will bring profound positive changes into your life. For me, it is all about inspiring you to power up your life with Divine Love. Divine, in this sense, means the highest vibration of love available. When we get out of our own way, when we choose to fill every cell, every subatomic particle of our being with Divine Love, we step into a life of miracles and magic. We literally flow with love, giving and receiving in balance.

Another secret to a healthy emotional life is to write down experiences from your exercises by journalling while they are fresh in your memory – how you felt before and how you feel now; truly celebrate the difference. Becoming your own healer, your own best friend, your own lover, your own partner, mother, and father, and doing the job the way you really want that job done is the true essence of soul empowerment that I coach and train my clients and students to achieve. Your life is down to you, and when you grab a hold of it and really jump on it, the world truly is your oyster.

There also needs to be detachment; don't make other people's dramas and lives your problem or challenge. You were given enough energy just for you and your life; you cannot fix anyone else or live their life for them. They came in with a whole host of lessons to learn, as did you.

The art of detachment helps you to still love them to bits but at the same time to stand back enough to let them learn by their own mistakes. This is one that mothers find challenging as there is, of course, a primordial desire to love your children so much you want to protect them from everything. Yet, what will strengthen their wings if you make it easy for them all the time? They won't become strong enough to fly on their own, so as you learn to self love and self-empower, as reading this book will undoubtedly help you do, you will be showing your children and grandchildren how it is done.

Teach by demonstrating, walking your walk, showing the way, not just talking a talk; that is easy. Make it happen by showing an inspiring example – what an amazing gift to give the young ones of today.

YOU are a gift to us all on the planet at this time. Remember that as you walk your path, with hopefully more awareness and love than perhaps you started out with before reading the words herein. Know and understand that life is a purposeful experience and just being who you are *is enough*. You are here to be happy and BE YOU and to remember who you truly are, a beloved soul, and a spiritual being having a human experience.

I am enough!

Affirm this often – it will make you feel great!

It has been a joy to put this chapter together for you. If I can help you in any way to self-heal and soul empower, please contact me on my website, info@patriciairiskerins.com and do befriend me on Facebook, Twitter or LinkedIn. My final words to you are 'Enjoy Being YOU'! This life passes quickly, in the twinkling of an eye; occupy your life well.

With much love, light and laughter,

Patricia Iris Kerins DHP June 2016

Star Mandala

Half a Lemon

Laura

I'M SITTING AT MY KITCHEN TABLE in the winter's energy and in the cold light of my life, surrounded by unpaid bills, feeling in that moment so disconnected from myself and questioning whether following my heart is a real act of self love or self-sabotage. I open up my kitchen cupboard to find half a packet of flour, a quarter jar of marmalade and a jiffy lemon! Oh yes, of course, there's an onion and another half a lemon in the fridge. My heart sinks as I realise my situation is not a conscious decision or because I have forgotten to do the weekly shop – I just don't have the money. This is a moment of truth for me, facing my inner beliefs about abundance, prosperity and money. My heart sinks further, as I see that although my singing and spiritual teaching life are blossoming, my songs being loved and bought by many people still, somewhere within me, I am storing an old belief of lack in my life. Now it is staring me squarely in the face – time for me to face my up to it.

In those desperate moments, thoughts of not being good enough as a mum, not being the provider that my daughter deserved, even feelings of deep guilt and shame overwhelmed me. I felt so inadequate despite being a passionate, conscious, devoted-to-her-life's calling, educated woman with a master's degree and certificates to prove it! All this meant nothing as I realised my being in this place was not through conscious choice but was the sum total of thoughts and beliefs I had chosen to carry for years – that shocked and angered me even more. How could I have ever believed this was what I deserve in my life? How could I have let things get this far? I saw my daughter's face looking at me and knew that all I have ever wanted is to give her the best. Those moments faced with feeding a hungry teenager brought me into a place of despair. But I knew that I could only surrender to a deeper level of faith in my dreams and life, to choose to turn my life around and empower myself to create a new heartset and mindset of abundance, self love and acceptance as a treasured gift to us both.

Changing didn't mean doing the same old things that had led me to this point; it meant completely rehashing and shifting my mindset around what I believed to be abundance and prosperity. I will be ever grateful for this pivotal moment, a shift I am still mastering as I turn that corner with love and kindness to myself. In those times of despair, looking at the onion but real tears rolling down my face, I vowed to myself and to Spirit within me that I would be the best I could be by loving and accepting myself as *enough* in all ways, by opening to be the vessel for *giving* from my heart. I knew this would enable me to provide whatever she and I deserve and that I would bring those messages of self love to those who cross my path, uplifting consciousness towards self-belief on this planet.

Of course, there were other things going on too, just to tip the scales and test my faith in myself and my God within me. Why not? Life likes setting a challenge! Along with her new found teenage freedom, my daughter started expressing her desire for independence by dismissing my role as her mother. What a combo! As if I wasn't working through enough. This led me to another gift of repairing and healing an older wound that I had pushed aside for many years: to find deeper forgiveness for myself and my daughter's father. This ran deep, it wasn't about the money at all.

Letting Go

Journeying deeper into embracing spiritual principles for my life, looking at myself in ways that empower me to change and heal what I don't like, letting go of blame, shame and self-deprecation and realigning with new habits and beliefs, all these have been a massive part of my learning and knowing deep in my heart that I *am* enough; that all I've ever done and am doing now is the best I can at the time. Forgiveness is my greatest key to believing I have choices, I can change *me*, I can apply new thoughts and beliefs, learn new habits that support me and build anew from past experiences with true forgiveness and no judgement.

If there is one thing you can embed in your heart and mind right now, it's that YOU DO WRITE THE STORY. In every single moment that exists, the choice is yours and with a new script comes a letting go and healing the old one; we often don't see old habits that we are wrapped up in, just repeating thoughts and beliefs and actions without consciously questioning ourselves. My deeper understanding is that true forgiveness is the trigger to releasing stale baggage and creating space for newness, and I feel guided to tell you that *daily* forgiveness for yourself and others is the key to a life filled with love, abundance, joy and deep inner peace. In her book, *The Four Spiritual Laws of Prosperity*, Edwene Gaines tells us that all financial lack is a sign of unforgiveness, debt is society's way of accepting pain, and pain is the outer effect of guilt... to explain this further what she teaches is that if we remain in a state of unforgiveness we are blocking life's energy for goodness which includes all abundance; financial debt is life's way of telling us that there's a lot of tired emotion to clear but with self-forgiveness we clear our hearts, opening up to love. Edwene sees financial debt as an opportunity to transform our lives by releasing old burdens that can block our heart space and financial flow. Life wants you to succeed, more importantly to be fulfilled, self-expressed, realise your worth and have the determination to change your mind and heartset. You can turn anything around no matter what you see as the obstacle, because it's your gift to look within and step dynamically over barriers with love and deep forgiveness.

Letting go in the midst of pain is the bravest and most loving act for spiritual unfolding, our relationships, and health on all levels. Forgiveness is certainly the key to my strength to allowing great things into my life. Why would we choose to hang on to old grudges and grievances living in a sense of frustration with ourselves, a certain person, place or thing and generally bring on feelings of discord, resentment, anger and fear? You see, staying in unforgiveness is a choice we make, to stick it out because of wanting a sense of control, having to be right, being fearful of backing down or softening our heart, not wanting to make the first move. Living with unforgiveness is in itself a trap we create for ourselves, to keep us bound to a person or situation. But we have a choice and we can create harmony and healing in our lives simply by releasing the event, person or situation and letting go with unconditional love. You can *unchoose* this choice at any time, there are no rules.

Forgiveness releases us from the chains of ourselves and from another person's energy or intention, allowing us to move on. They might not move on, but it isn't about them... it's about you. Self-forgiveness is always at the top of the list because it's vital to take full responsibility for the part we play in the tapestry of situations – there is always another side to the story. I often feel anger and frustration in the moment and yet I have realised over the years that hanging on to things that push my buttons, or getting upset over and over again doesn't fix a thing! The biggest fixer for me is FORGIVENESS and, as I deepen my daily practice of releasing it, I feel my heart opening up and love bringing an understanding of life that heals everything. Now I willingly look each day for where and who I can forgive and intentionally make this part of my enriched daily spiritual practice and I feel blessed to be at a place in my life where I am openly willing to do this. To let go, grow and heal.

The Sacred Labyrinth was my path to deep forgiveness, though I realise that all our journeys are different and we each find our way as we need to. Through willingness to forgive myself and others, a golden gateway of major healing opened up, zooming me into a place where I knew that letting go lovingly was the only way to move on.

As I continue to forgive I grow into the new me that I am becoming, it's a wondrous and magical journey which is here for you too, right now. There are many surprising ways to bring about forgiveness. The two that I find most powerful are here for you to enjoy.

Sweet Dreams Forgiveness Ritual

What we think and feel as we drop off to sleep impresses on our subconscious mind and becomes part of the reality we wake up to and chose to live by. I recommend that each person on the planet goes to sleep with good thoughts, including gratitude and forgiveness, whatever our outer experience might be at the time. Sleep is such an empowered time to do forgiveness work. The end of the day is a great opportunity for releasing, letting go of the energy of waking hours, to refresh and renew into a *new* day that awaits us...

- ♥ As you lay your head down gently and close your eyes serenely, tell yourself how you love and accept yourself – this is so important.
- ♥ Place the person/people/situation that you are ready to forgive in your heart, as you close your eyes and tell them they are loved and you are ready and willing to forgive them now.
- ♥ Ask if you can hug them or hold their hand as you forgive and feel your love pass to them in peace.
- ♥ Tell them *what* you are forgiving them for as you release the embrace and walk away with love.

- Know that you are both doing the best you can – acknowledge to yourself how loved you are.
- As you drift into sleep, hold thoughts and feelings of love – envelop yourself in bright white or violet light for knowing comfort. You can always repeat this exercise and hold great space for love in your heart.

It can feel challenging not to allow old thoughts to take over, stopping the flow of letting go; simply acknowledge this and, in your own time, affirm that you are ready and willing to release, forgive and move on.

Ho'ponopono Forgiveness Ritual

Ho'ponopono, the ancient Hawaiian forgiveness ritual, is beautiful and can deeply connect you to a place of letting go with unconditional love. It goes like this.

I am sorry

Please forgive me

I love Me – I love You

I let go.

Repeating this ancient wisdom chant over and over as you visualise peace within yourself and with any person or situation, is a blessing. Dynamic healing happens when you let yourself forgive and release pent up feelings, remember always to forgive yourself first, direct from your heart.

Divine Release, a song on my latest album, is a really useful tool for you to use when forgiving yourself and others, to attain a deep letting go. Use it daily to refresh your feelings about all sorts of experiences and situations; when used with love and meaning – it works!

Squeeze It

My lemon experience has been the biggest blessing for me as it was a growth spurt like no other, from which I am still growing and learning. As it unfolds, and I'm living through it, I find myself in a strengthened light that empowers me to continue in faith and belief of my calling: as a mama on a mission, as a soul empowerment singer and songwriter, as a spiritual student and teacher and as the best mum that I can be. I invite YOU to continue with whatever you deeply believe in your heart to be your highest calling for this life and to *go for it*, whatever your perceived obstacles may be. You see, living through this gives me the greatest opportunity to re-address my life through reshaping my thoughts and beliefs, and this is what it's all about: having a willingness to change. It's only when things get to a place where we feel completely unsafe, that we can pull up and reshift. Life gives us the opportunity to do this through the gift of *big* obstacles.

I know that the path isn't always easy or comfortable; but once we take that first step there is no turning back. Yes, there are still times that the kitchen cupboards have been on the spacious side but, each time, I choose to grow and to strengthen the faith in my calling – to love what I am doing and who I am.

Have you ever been in this place? Can you recall a time, or maybe you are living it now, feeling so broken and not knowing where to turn? Believing that nothing could ever change? It may be around money, relationships, health, children's choices. This is why I am here now, to let you know and show you how you can create change for yourself and your life. Not by trying to make everyone else the target, blame them or get angry when things don't work your way, simply to look at what's going on within you and turn your mind and heart-set around to a place of knowing that you are the power and you need do no more than surrender to that power and learn simple tools for using it, as if it were a magic wand. Look at your life and imagine yourself with any situation that's around you now, one you're not feeling 100% happy with. Know that you *can* make changes. Yes, for this to happen there is work involved; not outer work, it is an inner shifting. That's a commitment and yet it's wrapped as a golden gift of strength and faith to carry on.

It's only when we reach what we think is rock bottom that we can know in deep faith that we are *always* standing on solid ground and from there we can get up and walk with confidence to keep going on, listen up and fulfil our desires. It takes enormous faith, determination and belief in yourself, which is where self love comes in big time – be honest and true to the truth of you. By asking the golden question,

'How can I grow from this situation, right now?'

This can inspire you to understand deeply what life is giving you and the lemons you can squeeze for your own delicious overflowing jug full of sparkling *lemonaid*.

I can't give you the answer, no one can, because we each have our own bundle to unwrap with love as I do daily. However, I can share tools I have used and cherished, and still use daily, for you to know that you are safe, all is well and you are loved beyond measure.

Surrender Again

At the age of fifty-two, I made a vow to myself and to the divine within me, that I was now ready to allow myself to expand my consciousness, and to realise in my heart the power that I am. To do this I also realised that the road leads back to a glorious place, often visited and always revered, the place of SURRENDERING to LOVE. Yes, to where I know myself as e*nough*, as a mum, as a creative woman oozing with ideas and an excitement to bring them out into life, knowing that it's okay to relearn about money, finance and business. I allow and accept myself for just who I am and not to put myself down for not having skills, ones I didn't learn in the beginning; to learn these skills can be one enormous, creative, journey of fun and discovery. What I realise more and more is that there really is no separation from money, love, energy, and *me* and that I am the richness and prosperity of my life. Here, my message to you is to affirm within yourself that you are the key to all the locks. On realising your true power, and the love that you are, your whole world can shift in a flash.

Circles of life mandala

Eat Like You Give a Damn

Belle Amatt

WHILST PONDERING A TITLE FOR THIS PIECE an image flicks up onto my Instagram account, 'Eat Like You Give a Damn About Yourself' stares at me like a timely beacon and the tone is set.

21st Century living is fast-paced, offering the potential for a jam-packed journey full of wonderfully stimulating experiences. But if we are not fully fuelled and functioning optimally, remaining in fifth gear can become tricky. We may then start to flag, and when we flag, life is not quite so much fun. At this point, something has to give and this is often the quality and quantity of our meal times.

Food is not my friend right now is a phrase which I hear routinely in my practice. For various reasons women may have fallen out of love with feeding themselves or perhaps they have fallen in love with the wrong types of food. The pressures of modern day living can often revive buried neuroses around diet. When stress is high and our barriers are down it is not so easy to ride the wave of controlled adult eating. Reverting to being a picky eater, a binge eater or adopting a Paleo or gluten-free diet is often employed as a way to gain control over a life which is so demanding and tough to direct.

As women we are hard-wired to care for others whether we are looking after partners, nurturing children or caring for older relatives. We will often put others' needs before our own. The reasons for this are wide-ranging and may be based on our own childhood experiences, may be tied up in our gender role-modelling or be entirely down to circumstantial necessity.

As a nutrition consultant I am forever looking for causative factors, as identifying these often pave the way to workable solutions. So, to offer a route forward, I have identified three common scenarios which women may connect with: the emotion feeder, the starver and the role-model. In this way the development of each circumstance may be explored individually thereby allowing for more targeted tips.

1. The Emotion Feeder

Food can be a real crutch. We may turn to food when we are feeling down, elated, exhausted, stressed or, and here's one I relate to well... accomplished.

I was five, it was my first day at school and I was terribly nervous. On leaving me at the gates to the playground my mother winked and whispered, 'If you are good, I'll bring you a KitKat at the end of the day.' Throughout the day, I had lots of wobbly moments but I kept strong. I thought that if I cried then that wasn't being 'good' and would certainly cancel out the resulting chocolate bar. At 3pm, I was thrilled to have got through the day and sure enough, was greeted at the school gates with my sweet reward. The message stuck – 'master your fears, achieve and eat sugar.'

The significance here is not that we should blame our parents for individual weaknesses but that if we can look back and think *I can find a reason for feeling like this,* then we have the potential to work our way through it. On a personal level, I now recognise this pattern. At times when I am high-fiving myself for a day well accomplished, I know that a deep seated expectation for sugar will ensue. But I am prepared in true girl-scout style, having planned for this eventuality. There is no room for spontaneity when a sugar hit is a given. Therefore, I will have pre-made a tray of date bliss-balls or, if time is short, shopped wisely for sugar-free but satisfying nibbles. This may include a moderate amount of dried pineapple or mango alongside a small handful of nuts. I know, it's certainly a far cry from a KitKat but will serve my adult tastes for sugar.

Emotional eating to satisfy feelings of sadness can also be connected with our upbringing. As a parent it is a very natural reaction to feed an upset child. Most children in the depths of disappointment, loneliness or upset will react well to a parent or carer cooking them their favourite meal. And what might their favourite meal be? This is unlikely to involve that rocket and tomato salad which the parent has worked hard to incorporate as part of their five a day. More likely, the comfort food will comprise some heavy carbohydrates, cheesy pasta or a pizza maybe. It could well be followed with ice-cream or a stodgy pudding; anything to pacify the raw emotion. Remember that the food has been cooked and served with love so the emotional associations will be strong.

Translated into a grown-up scenario of comfort eating, it is clear why, if this is our own story, we will be reaching for soothing carbohydrates in times of sorrow. In our memories, such a food fix is connected to feelings of love and support.

But what are we really after? It is perhaps the *comfort* part of the comfort eating which is required. Ask yourself if this is achievable by accessing reassurance through a different channel; this could be a conversation with the person closest to you, a walk in the fresh air, a yoga session or tuning in to a mindfulness app. Whatever works best. In this way you are acknowledging the cause of your food association and turning it into something positive which works well for you, rather than against you.

Exhaustion can also set the scene for mindless eating but this is likely to have physiological roots rather than the familial behaviour we have considered so far. Food is fuel, undoubtedly so when we are running on vapours, hunger is inevitable.

All food is turned to glucose and used in different ways by our body. We need to eat regular meals to keep ourselves topped up. As many of us are office bound performing mind based tasks or spending many hours in creative thought, let's consider the requirement of the brain.

The brain uses up around twenty percent of our daily calories. It commands a constant supply of glucose which it prefers in the form of carbohydrates (fruits, vegetables, grains etc.). Only when deprived of this favoured fuel will the brain use other substances. Therefore we need to be able to spot the signs of low blood glucose and act on them quickly. Confused thinking, light headedness, shakiness, anxiety and irritability are all symptoms which may be linked to a lack of glucose. It is tempting to work straight through these sensations especially if they have become part of your normal routine. However, ignoring the signs is only going to lead to a frantic eating situation later that day. Would you ignore the warning light on your fuel gauge? Of course not, as this would lead to a breakdown. So we need to apply the same principles to our own personal energy tank.

Preferable to waiting for these signs in order to eat is to avoid the symptoms in the first place. Identify your problem areas by thinking through what exactly is going wrong. Is it the food type, the missed meals, the lack of foods? This of course is where the beauty of a bespoke consultation lies as each individual has their own areas for improvement, which may not be immediately obvious. For a more DIY approach, I suggest keeping a food diary and noting down when and what you eat and drink, and times when you feel any of the above mentioned symptoms. This will give you clear clues as to what you may be doing wrong. Aim for three meals per day, breakfast being within one hour of waking, lunch at a set time (noon is great for a 9-5 work regime) and eat your final meal an hour before bed. To get a decent night's sleep we need to be digesting our food before we fall into bed.

Hone in on food types too for better energy levels. All meals should contain the major food groups, carbohydrates, protein and fats. Living on carbs is quick and easy but may lead to energy slumps post lunch. What we need is a nice, steady drip feed of blood glucose to keep us going for the duration of the day. This should avoid those exhaustion led cravings which can tempt us into the biscuit barrel.

Stress led eating can often manifest in bingeing. Again this is generally due to a physical reaction linked to the release of stress hormones. In generally calm living, a touch of stress can actually be quite functional. That rise and fall of adrenaline may push us forward to get things done by upping our pace. It is the on-going chronic stress which may lead to disordered eating. If you recognise this pattern then getting to the root of the stress or learning how to manage stress more proficiently could help to reduce a propensity to binge eat.

In our frenzied, fast-paced world, it is the consistent release of the stress hormone, cortisol which may be triggering cravings for salty, sweet, and fatty foods. For those in the category of healthy, serene and free of on-going anxiety the hormone cortisol, released by the adrenal glands, troughs and peaks to a diurnal rhythm. Generally it peaks in the morning to awake us, then drops as the day continues and allows us to fall asleep at bedtime.

'Cortisol is the hormone which wakes us up in the morning,' I once explained to a client.

'No, I think you'll find that is my alarm clock,' she replied looking exhausted.

For those who relate to these words, finding it a tough call to pull themselves out of bed and find the inclination to start the day, it could well be that a constant release of cortisol in reaction to stress could be contributing to those feelings of lethargy.

In short term stressful situations, cortisol is brilliantly useful, preparing the body for a fight-or-flight response by increasing available fuels (the production of new glucose is stimulated within the body). This gives us quick-fix fuel for the muscles and brain to respond to the stressful incident. We can use this to our advantage to run for that train, snatch a child from being mowed down by a cyclist or up the ante on a 5K run.

Unfortunately, in chronic stress, cortisol has many disadvantages including its effect on appetite and cravings for high-calorie foods. A direct association has been made during studies in populations of women (1), between cortisol levels and calorie intake. Therefore, if you are a stress eater it is vital to break the cycle in order to regain a level of control around food. The first step is identifying the fact that you feed stress and understanding that the root of this is physiological. The root can now be addressed by taking steps to manage stress and to re-stabilise the rhythm of your cortisol release.

For clients who like a piece of data to work with I often use a saliva test in order to measure levels of cortisol. This allows us to see exactly what is happening; is the pattern entirely disordered, is the hormone peaking wildly or are the adrenal glands flagging so listlessly that cortisol has hit an all-time low? Functional testing offers a great tool to support bespoke nutrition. However without this data we can still work on some stress-busting techniques to avoid using food as a coping mechanism. This is a two-pronged approach, firstly to cope better with the stress of 21st century living and secondly to avoid adding any further dietary stress. See the end of the chapter for some appetite balancing ideas.

2. The Starver

It is essential that I am extremely clear here. This section is not a discussion on eating disorders, for this is beyond the scope of my chapter. Here I offer advice for women whose hunger is generally over-ridden by other elements of their life.

For some it's plain and simple: they forget to eat. This seems extraordinary to the foodies amongst us but the truth is that not everyone is motivated by food. Work tasks and deadlines can often prevail over hunger. The starver can get so stuck into a project that it consumes their headspace upon waking, causing the omission of breakfast. They may well then plough right through until dinner giving not a solitary thought to refuelling.

For others it is not about being busy, more of apathy around food. Meal times perhaps are just not on their radar. If family meals did not feature in childhood then having set meal times is unlikely to be rolled out in adult life. This brings us back to role modelling and the great importance of recognising dysfunctional eating patterns and working through them, thus breaking the cycle.

Adopting special diets such as the Paleo, gluten free or fasting programmes may also develop the 'starver' persona. I'm not opposed to food fads provided they are used for well-being. Fashions and trends around foods are often criticised for creating catastrophe at meal-times, however food fads can also raise awareness around healthy eating so I feel we need to strike a balance. The avoidance of certain food triggers, especially gluten and dairy, for those with genuine intolerances can truly improve their health. However, it is crucial that these regimes are followed for the right reasons.

Using a food fad to further restrict the diet in a fussy eater is certainly a destructive measure and needs to be worked through. If this is ringing true then it is vital to recognise it fully and look carefully at your diet to keep it well-balanced. Understanding the potential dangers of being a 'starver' may offer a level of motivation which initiates change.

Chronic meal skipping will lead to under-performance in work and home life. Our 21st century existence is tough enough without starving the brain of the glucose it needs to keep going. Your brain's supply of glucose becomes compromised within four to six hours of your last meal or snack (2), so stop to consider the challenge we are putting ourselves under by starving the brain for long periods. Memory, attention levels and mental performance are surely suffering but it is difficult to comprehend this when we cannot think straight enough to recognise it happening.

So you may be wondering how on earth the starver manages to keep going throughout the day having skipped breakfast and lunch – it may be around eighteen hours since the last meal! Ketosis may step in. This is a process in which the body metabolises fat for energy once its stored carbohydrates are used up. This is not an appealing fat burning situation. Its negative side-effects include nausea, constipation, tiredness, tax on the kidneys and low blood pressure. On a consistent basis, the body will adapt to burn fewer calories, will put the brakes on metabolism, cling to fat stores and decrease lean muscle tissue. This is why I see many 'starvers' who cannot reach their preferred weight as the body just won't let go of the fat.

For the 'starver' situation, it is time to re-evaluate. I have offered the mechanics of why skipping meals is detrimental to health but how about emotionally? Could we pause for a moment amidst the chaos of our days, anchor our feet to the ground, close our eyes and just consider a simple question – *why*? We all have choices; daily we prioritise, often working our way triumphantly down the *what to do* list, commending ourselves on our accomplishments at the end of a bountiful day. But *why* do we forget or omit to feed ourselves regularly on a daily basis. Should this not be at the top of our lists?

The truth is that caring for ourselves is often overlooked. Generally we observe our parents caring for us and nourishing us (to whatever extent this may happen within a family). This ritual is then passed down to our children. But unless it is directly stated, do children understand the importance of looking after themselves? Seemingly not; consider how many young adults go to university or leave home with no cooking skills and an aversion to washing. Caring for oneself is a notion that may be considered selfish or egocentric in our society. It is the reason why food fads are often ridiculed as 'first world issues'. There is a certain animosity towards looking at the self too deeply.

Do you recall that Brownie Guide Law, "A Brownie Guide thinks of others before herself and does a good turn every day"? Robert Baden-Powell has left this motto firmly inscribed on the minds of many. Of course, this is a hugely positive motto to have imprinted on one's psyche but my point is I do not recall anyone ever drumming into me, 'Eat like you care and look after your health or you'll be too knackered to think of others and too strung out to help anyone'.

So what is my advice here for those identifying with the 'starver'? Look to Hippocrates who coined the phrase *Food is Medicine* to express how eating healthy and nourishing food is at the basis of good physical and emotional health. We only get one shot at this wonderful life so why would we deprive ourselves of the vital fuel we need in order to live deeply and with the greatest longevity we can muster. Whatever your schedule, your profession or your situation there is always room to modify the diet in order to optimise your day. If short of food preparation time, on a budget or in a state of food apathy then find yourself a food blogger who suits your needs. Make a weekly food planner made up of easy to construct healthy dishes. There are so many books out there instructing us how to concoct a healthy meal in under an hour, within thirty minutes or even ten. It's all there for you from this whirl of total information we exist within, so use this to your advantage.

Let the foodie fanatics do the thinking for you and simply follow their lead. It couldn't be easier in this day and age. Social media can be an inspiring friend! Be enthused by foodie photographs and daily posts from your chosen food blogger. Instagram is perfect if you are a visual being. Find here a colourful stimulus to fuel your food planner with new and exciting recipes, look to seasonal fruit and vegetables to increase those essential nutrients we need to keep us not only existing but living to the full.

My overall message in this section: EAT. Not because you are ravenously hungry. Not because there just happens to be food in front of you. But eat with purpose and intention. Eat with the same drive that you offer other sections of your life. Some drink champagne, invest heavily in their wardrobes, purchase only the finest food for their pets or acquire the most up to date gadgets. These wants and desires are handled with passion. And this is all fine. But let us invest passionately in our health too. Eat because you really care about being alive.

You are worth more than the occasional Quality Street.

3. The Role-Model

"Parenthood: ... a colossal undertaking."

This quotation is taken from the first chapter of my novel *Balloon Girl*. *Balloon Girl* is contemporary women's fiction: it is a tale charting the lives of a mother and daughter, and commenting on role-modelling, intricate family relationships and self-acceptance.

The mothers amongst us strive to be good role models. But as Anna, the older protagonist in the novel points out, what we really need is a handbook to talk us through it. Without this we tend to either feel our way through, reacting to our child's individual behaviour at a spontaneous level or turning to our own parents' child-rearing codes which do not always lend themselves to 21st century living.

In this section I am going to offer my experience of how to create a good eater. But of equal importance, I will move on to a crucial point – do not let your own health flag in the process of child-rearing. The value of *self-care* is vital!

I commonly hear stories of parents striving to create 'good eaters'. This is often an area of much stress as children will naturally define their personalities by choosing foods or other items which they do or do not like. There is a theory that between eighteen months and two years of age fear of new foods creeps in – termed 'neophobia' literally meaning 'fear of the new'. Evolutionary psychologists have traced this back to the cave-dwelling period (3). They suggest that such fussy tendencies would have discouraged young children from ingesting newly encountered and potentially poisonous plants. Indeed research has shown that it is the very foods we most want children to eat – fruit and vegetables – that are most often rejected at this stage (4).

Regardless of the background, it is a hugely frustrating time for parents as failed attempts to role-model healthy eating end up flicked onto the carpet. Frequently such behaviour is reacted to with familiar patterns of coercion, bribery or anger (possibly role-modelled by our own parents). These reactions can quickly develop into a battleground of fledgling temper tantrums versus adult logic. The two do not gel. What we require is the delivery of calm and methodical meals eaten with joy and enthusiasm.

How to create the good eater? Decide on tolerance and perseverance and stick to these principles. Your child may turn their nose up at a certain food or tell you outright that they do not want it on their plate. How you react, as a parent or carer may well pave the way for how your child decides to eat throughout childhood. So, without wanting to exert too much pressure, I do believe it is important to get this right.

My own experience went like this:

My first child ate anything. In fact I indulged the delightful fact that she would eat anything and she became a big eater with little appetite control. I recognised my mistake and managed to rein this in by the time she reached ten. My second child was an entirely different challenge. As soon as she could hold a spoon her belligerent little self decided that she would eat nothing from it. In fact, she would eat nothing from a bowl or a plate. Any food presented on either was immediately turned upside down and shaken onto the floor. She would eat with her hands but only whilst sitting on the floor picking food off a plastic sheet. Could it get any trickier? I sensed that remaining calm was essential and took to reading widely on fussy kids. I tried all techniques offered, praying that I would hit on the right one for my child before my own patience dwindled.

There was no quick-fix. I took to inspiring her in as many ways as I could fathom. Always eating the same food together, sitting calmly at the table we spent endless meal times with me making overly enthusiastic 'this is yummy' sounds whilst she listened, wide-eyed, propelling cherry tomatoes across the room. With as much belligerence as she (I acknowledge the hereditary characteristics), I took to growing these detested tomatoes, giving her the role of plant waterer with her dinky pink watering can. And this was the moment when patience paid off.

With her first tiny, ripe, home-grown tomato the foodie light-bulb moment occurred – 'ping'. I would never have imagined that she would pick it straight off the plant and pop it into her mouth, eating the fruit with a squeal of delight.

What had happened, I believe, is that she had associated food with fun, with nature and time spent in a happy and calm setting. She had disassociated food with misbehaving as the reaction she was after just wasn't forthcoming.

Be persistent and don't expect immediate results. Coercion, bribery and anger give off the wrong message. Healthy food should not be a stepping stone to an ice-cream or a way to get your pocket money. Anger at meal times may lead to an unpleasant relationship with food in later life so is best avoided. Life should be about love, food and respect for others and these three essentials need to tie in together.

As a role-model working on creating the good eater, please spare a thought for yourself. As I have mentioned, in our society there is more emphasis on looking after others and little on self-care. We live and die for our children, caring deeply that they have the best experience of childhood. Keep a close eye on your own health. The stress of worrying about others can be extremely detrimental and it is vital that we practice a level of, what shall we call it – self-preservation? I feel this fits.

We live in a fast paced, work centred world in which, as women, we may feel a mountain of pressures which on a day to day basis do not even surface as conscious thought. These may include the need to fulfil the potential of that university degree which your parents worked so hard to fund. The spinning plates of motherhood, the supportive partner, the caring friend and the actively sociable profile on your social media settings are often part of your unbridled normality.

Step away for a moment, take a deep breath and check you are feeling good, in optimal health, sleeping well and, if nothing else, EAT LIKE YOU GIVE A DAMN.

Fusion

This chapter describes three separate personas and you may well be gelling with one of them or maybe more than one.

However I would like to fuse together these personalities in order to create one overall constructive message and that is to recognise where making positive changes could enhance your wellbeing; both emotional and physical wellbeing. I have, along the path of life, experienced all of these personas and learnt so much from them. By identifying the emotional and physiological habits of the 'emotion feeder' I have worked towards change, stability and balance with clients. By understanding and teaching the physiological implications of the 'starver' I have offered the motivation required to prioritise regular meals for the mind and the body.

On a personal level, such an understanding of balanced nutrition has enabled a calmer and more attentive outlook, a more tolerant disposition, tranquillity and compassion. This calm allows for patience and resilience when role-modelling and offers a more focussed awareness of one's own health and vitality. Work towards it and you will notice results in the ability to remain mentally and physically alert, to fall asleep with ease and to remain asleep. To wake feeling refreshed. To achieve and strive with way more energy and resolve.

Most fulfilling is to watch your kids watching you and, by their actions, to know that you are getting it right.

My Tips for Balanced Eating

For appetite control aim for mindful eating with plenty of chewing, regular mealtimes, foods low in sugar, meals rich in protein and fibre, daily exercise and stress busting meditation or yoga. The three tips below add a bit of rationale on how to achieve a more balanced approach to eating in an often unbalanced world.

Be Militant about Breakfast

- By daybreak our liver glycogen stores start to fade and blood glucose levels decline. To keep blood glucose in range, cortisol starts to rise peaking first thing in the morning as mentioned. If we eat breakfast then we are supplying the glucose required to allow cortisol to taper off and relinquish its role in the production of glucose.
- Find a breakfast which you look forward to and make this a key part of your morning ritual. Make it nourishing and make it work for you. I often hear 'I don't have time for breakfast' or 'I just want something I can pour out of a cereal box'. But let's *make* time for breakfast knowing that it is so important for allowing us to cope well and sail through our day rather than paddling upstream.

Limiting Caffeine and Alcohol

The whys and wherefores

Both these stimulants act as a crutch in periods of stress but we need to reassess. We cannot always control our external stressors but we can ensure that we do not add to these by over consuming these two well-known nutrient drainers. Moderation is required unless our adrenals have really hit the ground, in which case it would be wise to omit them entirely. We all know this, but actioning it is a different matter. I suggest making a plan. If you are a coffee-head then wean off gently and decide on your realistic goal: this could be two cups per day. Decide which ones you love the most. This is often the morning cup of coffee. I get it entirely. Coffee lovers are often keen on ritual, the loading of grains or the frothing of milk and if this is what gets you out of bed then stick with it, but eat first.

Caffeine is addictive, its regular use causing mild physical dependence so it's wise to prepare for the fact that you will be craving a hit. Replacing your regular coffee moments with green or white tea offers an anti-oxidant rich, less caffeinated option which psychologically will help with the substitution.

Moderate alcohol use has been known to reduce stress due its sedative properties but for chronic stress the addictive tipple needs to be approached with caution. Habits form with such ease, especially in a society in which the use of alcohol is widely condoned. There are a million excuses to open the bottle: it's a Friday night, I'm cooking a risotto, the kids have misbehaved, there are work celebrations, Thursday is the new Friday, someone's birthday... The truth is it is always someone's something and while we are creating a plan to eat because we care, then alcohol has to be trickling rather than flowing.

Continuous consumption of alcohol over an extended period of time has been shown to raise the levels of cortisol in the body and we are trying to avoid this. Plan your consumption and stick to it. Define a non-food reward scheme if this is what motivates you. Pay yourself for glasses not poured or bottles unbought. Focus on how fantastic it feels once you begin to regain your handle on stress. If we are after a direct link between over-eating and alcohol to motivate us then consider the recent research on how women's brains react to food aromas when under the influence. One study found that alcohol consumption enhanced the brain's sensitivity to external food cues, such as aromas, and led to increased food consumption

(5). This has been labelled the *aperitif* effect. Many will relate to that overwhelming desire for food after a few alcohol drinks; well now we know it has been researched and documented we can add this to our reasons for practising moderation.

Eat Together

Shared mealtimes are valuable on many levels. As we pause to converse, we chew and swallow. We stop to chuckle at shared moments. What may have seemed black spots to the day become, with hindsight, moments of hilarity, now shelved. We digest. We wind down. We relate.

With shared meals, as long as they are approached with calm and tolerance, comes better digestion and emotional wellbeing. For those with children, role-modelling can be approached more effectively. For those without, shared meal times are equally beneficial for we are back to my overall feeling regarding food; that life is about love, food and respect for others.

REFERENCES:

1. Epel E, Lapidus R, McEwen B, Brownell K. Stress may add bite to appetite in women: A laboratory study of stress-induced cortisol and eating behavior. Psychoneuroendocrinology: 2001;26(1):37-49.

2. Tribole, E. Eating on the Run, 2003

3. Cooke, L et al, Genetic and environmental influences on children's food neophobia, 2007

4. Dovey, T et al, Food neophobia and 'picky/fussy' eating in children: A Review, 2008

5. Eiler W, et al. The apéritif effect: Alcohol's effects on the brain's response to food aromas in women. Obesity, Volume 23, Issue 7, pages 1386–1393, July 2015

Sacred geometry mandala

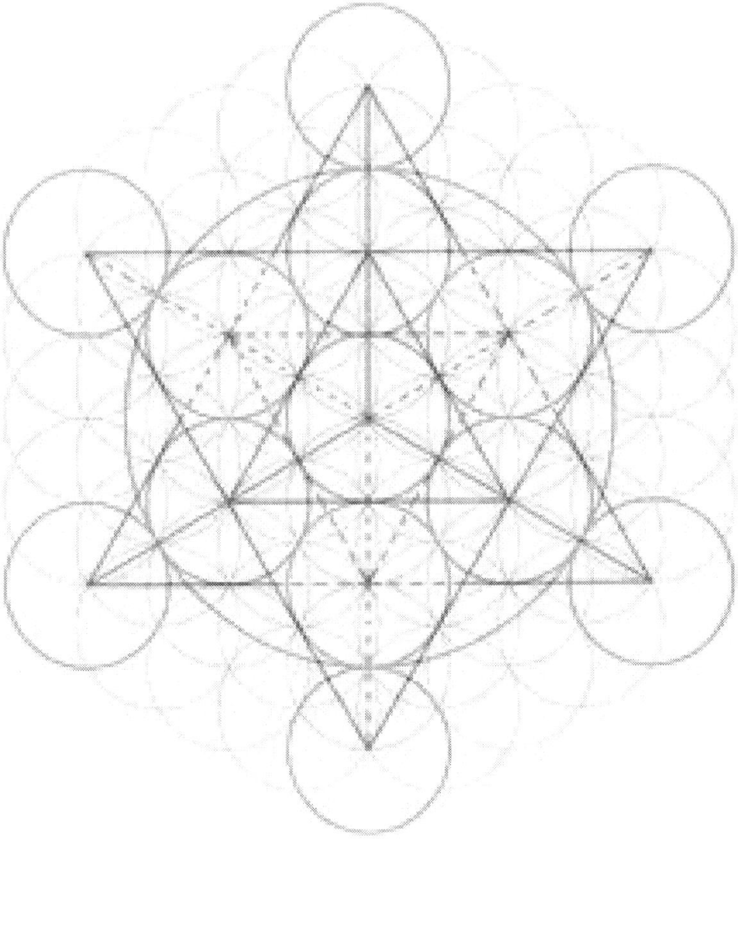

Sell-By Dates, Cooking the Stew

Lay your table fit for a queen

Laura

TV DINNER ON A TRAY or banquet in the great dining hall, how do you prepare your food; what's cooking on the stove to be served at your table? Just like our food prep, our thoughts and beliefs and how we talk to ourselves every moment affect the dish and it can be a fine line between enjoying the meal or throwing it in the bin. Spiritual food is the meal of our minds and its ingredients, our thoughts. Have you checked out that cupboard recently, you know the one where you keep the salt, pepper, seasonings and jars of stuff that make you feel in charge in the kitchen? Are all the products in date or is there a packet of cornflour from 2012 and an old salt refill pack from 2006?

It's the same with our inner cupboards; those shelves that store our thoughts, beliefs and unsupportive messages we so willingly give ourselves that can be out-dated and really unhelpful for our lives. It's time to clean up and clear out the cupboards! Regular letting go of those old condiments, refreshing the sauce bottles and, while you're at it, cleaning the shelves is what is called for to allow in a whole new variety of flavours. Your thoughts and beliefs, just like your cooking ingredients, are the bed rock for supporting your life and deserve the best atmosphere for storage, so take time and care to look at them regularly, question your need for them and let go and clean up where you can.

Watch what goes into the stew, prepare it with care and thought, stir gently with love and faith so that your meal will taste delicious every time. Vegan, veggie or full-on meat eater, it doesn't matter, it's all about the love care and faith that you put into your stew and the belief that as you're cooking it the juices and flavours are mixing together perfectly for your delicious meal. This dish is your creation, just like your life, and it's up to you to think carefully about how you want your life to be, the flavour you want to taste. Do you like mild easy to swallow mouthfuls or are you a hot, spicy mama in need of excitement and rhythm? Either way is great and it's for you to create it in your way. Go for it and really enjoy experimenting, always using fresh ingredients. State your values for life and live in your truth – it is vital for harmony and fulfilment. Know who you are and live it out as your desire. As you learn to draw the line for what you do and don't want for your life, you are preparing your delicacy.

Lay your table fit for a QUEEN. Because that, my friend, is what you are, the ruler of your world. Sit with power at the head of your table knowing what you lay out before you expresses pride, integrity, faith, authentic self love and care. Be ruler of *your* world, not your children's, partner's or friend's... make this your world and life and live it with absolute integrity as you build up, clear and set focussed intention to live in the values you uphold.

My treasured values are love, fulfilment (which is very different from success), forgiveness, abundance, a compassionate heart and gratitude. What are your top five values for living? Think about them, write them out and live by them every day. Stick them on your mirror, read them out in the morning and build those values into your life. This is your table, set for a queen, and you deserve no less than this.

In the Bedroom

The key to great sex? Only do it when you feel like doing it and do it with passionate LOVE

Yes, sex is a great thing to write about and it feels really liberating to spill out my thoughts about how, as women on top, we can often be underneath, metaphysically speaking! It's not through conscious choice, more through unconscious patterning, taking our habitual role as people pleaser into the bedroom. Now, don't get me wrong here, I'm not saying that we have to be in the mood in order to have sex, many a time I haven't felt like having sex but, without pressure from myself or partner, I've chosen to indulge my bodily lust and felt great about it. What I am talking about here is that often an act of sex is because we think it will please our partner so we say 'yes' to subconsciously keep the peace in the relationship, to fulfil an unspoken pact, or to feel more worthy because we then feel needed. I've been there and done it and it's a place filled to the brim with lack of self love. For years I chose to stay in a relationship built on love, yes, but also on my fear of a lack of financial security. My partner, a love addict, had it down pat, my low self love beam was glowing brightly and it kept me tied to a relationship centred around his sexual pleasure. Was this fulfilling for me? No. Was this a place that I really wanted to be? No. Was it nurturing for my soul? No, not at all. In fact it left me empty, living a lie to myself and full of feelings of helplessness deep within. On the day that I had a roast potato moment and nearly threw them over him in fury, I saw the light and decided to move on. This was the beginning of another phase of my life. I was giving myself another chance to be true to my deeper soul's calling. Letting go of a love that was not feeding me anymore, not knowing how I would survive emotionally or financially and yet driven to claiming back my self, my body, my power and coming through on the other side.

We know when it's right and, when it *is* right, it's not for any reason other than wanting to give and receive love through the body just because it makes us feel good; in this way we are loving ourselves and another. Having sex and mixing it with love is the greatest blend of physical, spiritual and emotional energy, so what's the point of half doing it? Do it with love with meaning and power; that really doesn't mean hanging from the chandelier, it's more about the feeling you arouse within yourself and the power behind that feeling. Sex is the greatest act of giving and receiving love for ourselves and our partner and it's here to be enjoyed, explored and embodied with loving fun and full on heartfelt passion.

It is right when we feel seated in our power of saying 'yes' or 'no' because when speaking and living our truth we are respected and regarded. It is right when we are mentally aligned with our partner and not feeling any sense of guilt, shame, having to do it: *I don't really want* to, or *okay, just this once*. It's right when we can do it ourselves and feel the power of that. It's all about the feeling with everything we do – if it's not feeling right then it's time to question, to go deeper, to decide where you draw the line in order to retain your power, to stay in your perimeter and ask, *Why is life giving me this situation, how can I heal and forgive through this now?* So, great sex is all about feeling GREAT not because of it, just because of YOU, and it is always enacted with LOVE – it's that simple.

Hi Vibe

Vibrating at Heaven Level?

Oh yes! When we choose to live in and send out good vibrations we are choosing to live in a complete STATE OF HEAVEN which, by the way, is not somewhere out there in the midst of the invisible. Heaven is right where you are and you can choose to drink from its infinite waterfall or stand at the edge and watch. Heaven is a complete state of being and as our hearts and minds grow into this understanding, we can learn to live in the constant vibration of what I call *heavenness*. The first thing to understand is that nothing outside ourselves is changeable, we can only be willing and ready to make changes within ourselves. We all know – we've tried to change them, we've got angry with them, *it's all his fault, it's all her problem*. However, that's just not how it works. We can change or control nothing other than our own thoughts, beliefs, feelings, words and actions, and that's it! Nothing else is changeable and that's the key to living in your power and giving yourself permission to shine. Living in your state of heavenness is your responsibility and begins with your thoughts and your vibe. Yes, it starts with you. Breathe in the goodness daily and as you claim your power you will see and feel your outer world changing. This is the art of being a *Mama on a Mission*.

D.I.Y.

Because You Can

If you want something done, do It yourself! I expect you know that old saying? Well, I've realised there's no truer expression. We are so conditioned by life to look outside ourselves for love, acceptance, gratification and approval but that can place tremendous impact on our self-belief, self-esteem and self love. It was an enormous turning point when I got it, I mean really understood that there's nothing outside myself that verifies my sense of worth and it's up to me to overflow with complete knowing that I will love and accept myself, my choices, my life, regardless of another's views about me. I stopped seeking approval from my partner, friends, family, social media and began asking, 'Is this my truth? Does this make me feel good? Is this a loving act? Do I love and approve of ME, just as I Am?'

Naturally, the answers were not always a resounding *Yes!* and the greatest thing about owning and taking responsibility for my choices was creating my very own setpoint of personal values and beliefs which I now work and align my desires with in building a clear picture of what I desire and expect for my life. I do it myself and as I leap into life, trusting my own feelings, I feel so empowered as I no longer ask anyone to verify my choices.

Getting past the point of being concerned what others think or feel about our choices is where the action happens. It's where real responsibility-taking kicks in and it's also where we can learn how to please and transform ourselves without relying on anyone else. Here is where we create life in the way it feels good for us and not create just for others; here we can be ourselves. It is tremendously liberating. Move over Women's Lib – turn on to Mama's Lib!

I recall being in a certain relationship years ago with a man who I believed loved me, but feeling so insecure that I allowed him to influence my sense of whether I was good enough. I gave all my power to him and sought his approval over and over so that, knowing this, he held me dangling on a string. I bless this man, as he taught me so much about stepping out and claiming my self-worth, however painful it was at the time, I learned a very big lesson from him, which was to disengage from his idea of my worth and to build my own solid *self*-worth structure within me, with foundations so deep that no one could ever again knock it down. This took time well spent and devotion to myself and was an exciting rediscovery of my beliefs about myself, my looks, my personality and my whole life. I was willing to lovingly and forgivingly let go of the old – yes that included my relationship with him – and to embrace the new by learning to love all that I Am, even parts that I once felt I disliked. Here's where I began and how you can too...

Get Your Tool Kit Out

- ♥ Begin by noticing and jotting down the things that you seek external approval for from your loved ones, friends, work colleagues...
- ♥ Next, become aware of and note the people you seek this approval from. Is there a pattern of those who are closest that you fall back on for reassurance?
- ♥ Now, imagine and repeat three times in your mind the answer that you would really like to hear from that person.

♥ Go to the mirror with that answer and tell it to yourself, out loud with real conviction and love, over and over, knowing that YOU ARE ENOUGH and you love and accept yourself unconditionally without seeking help from outside.

This may feel a little strange even uncomfortable at first, just stick with it, you are doing something new and this can be scary. But, once you are in the routine of this dynamic exercise you will feel and know that you only have to look to *yourself* for love, acceptance and reassurance.

As you practice this over and over you'll feel a building sense of self-assurance and those you would usually turn to for approval will also feel the ripple as you release your reliance on them and grow into a beacon of light for self-love, they will wonder why you don't need their acceptance – and this will shift your world!

Seeking approval from outside means you never truly live life in your own way. To live your own mission it is crucial to be reliant on asking only *one* person for the yes or no and that person is YOU. It's time to take charge, to live the life you want and to know that if things go belly-up there's only yourself to look to. I believe this is the most empowering part of all that I am learning and I invite you to collect yourself, acknowledge how fantastic you are and truly feel it from within, to a degree that you have confidence to keep going back to yourself for love, acceptance and approval of your next step. Mastering this is the way to discover your true power and it's a learning that, when mastered, can phenomenally change the way you handle yourself and your life.

So, begin by noticing your need for approval about smaller things; it astounds me how when I am shopping with my daughter there are times I turn to her for the *okay* on a top that I'm trying on! Hello, earth calling Laura! I'm a grown self-assured woman who has purchased many tops before she ever arrived, so why do I feel the need for her yea or nay about random clothes purchases? I don't, that's the truth, but still there are times when we feel the need to be approved of by our loved ones, society, friends, the entire world and it's exhausting because we can express greatness and difference, regardless of anyone else's opinion. I've learned that when she says no it's a great sign for me to buy it, and love it! So now's the time to bring awareness to being certain of yourself and to simply nurture your DIY tool kit.

Ask yourself:

- What you seek approval for
- Who you regularly turn to
- How you feel with the responses you are given

For each point take note and tell yourself over and over how you *love* and *accept* and *approve* of yourself – just as you are.

You Are More Than Enough! Where's the Money Honey?

When at the brink of complete money flow meltdown, find a quiet space, take three deep breaths – and scream.

This works wonders as a release, although it's probably not the longterm *soul*ution that can transform things and bring about oodles of spare cash, unless it's a part of a well paid theatrical act that you do on the side! Seriously, I believe that arriving at that roar of frustration and releasing it out loud can be so healing for the soul.

Trying to be a Nobel Prize mathematician and work out how to pay all the bills at the same time can be the most frustrating and heart wrenching experience. I know, I've been there and I might add, I'm still there. However, the difference between being there five years ago and being there now, is that I now have a whole beautiful kaleidoscope of tools that guide and show me that I don't have to work out what has already been worked out in the Divine. I use my own inner power and faith to recreate my reality and I do it in a very specific way. Basically, I trick my subconscious and reaffirm the truth, make a new reality as I let the old scene go with forgiveness and in *faith* and *belief*, that life is on my side. Am I really without the money that I think I should have, or am I experiencing life in such a way that it pushes me to grow, to believe in myself and step right out of my comfort zone into my power? This shift in perception is how I work now, and it all comes from within.

We know and we hear that money is energy, no more no less. How many times I've heard that one coming at me from books, on-line, in social media! I've known this for many years but it's not about knowing it in the mind, it's about feeling it in the heart – and living it.

That energy that everyone's talking about is *flow*, it's receptivity, it's unconditional love and most of all it is GIVING. Giving time to those we love, giving knowledge to those we can guide, giving a smile to those we feel compassion for, giving money to spiritual causes, giving love to ourselves, because if we're not in the flow of giving, accepting, receiving and allowing love into our lives, then how can we ever expect a huge red truck full of money to drop from the sky and land just perfectly on our doorstep?

To be in the flow you've got to *get* in the flow and that means giving and allowing the flow to flow through you. The key is that *we* are the money, there is no separation between us and flow, money and ideas, love and life. It's one inseparableness and when we flick the switch and realise this, not simply in the mind but in our heart, then we are in line for action. Look for the good there is around you now and live in that good which flows right in and through you. Feeling grateful is a wonderful place to begin, knowing that you are the abundance of life and that by embracing all the good where you are provides power to bring in more. Be your own flow.

Just like love, life and goodness, abundance is a state of heart and mind. Living in a state of prosperity consciousness takes a certain awareness and often a willingness to make great changes, not *out there* changes, it demands more subtle shifts and choices that have their roots in thoughts and beliefs that we simply carry with us subconsciously. Having the desire to transform, from where you are right here and now, is the opening key to being your own pot of gold. This might mean looking honestly and deeply at your thinking around money patterns – how you view your story or deservability; however strange or uncomfortable it may seem to do this, by to unearthing the blockages you can create a life full of prosperity in ways you could never imagine possible.

Housekeeping – Leaky Tap Syndrome

The tap's leaking, it's dripping into the cupboard and now the shelf is rotten.

To fix the rotten shelf in the cupboard we have to look at the leaky tap as the cause and make direct changes. Getting a new shelf will not solve the issue until a new washer is fitted to the tap. This is how life works: if we continue trying to fix the outer effect without going to the root, the tap will just keep on dripping

Our house is our home and our place of being, living, expressing, resting and nurturing. It is a deep and mirrored reflection of us in all ways. Metaphysically speaking our house is our body, our outer, our physical, the thing that we know of as the system of humanness and life. As wonda mamas we travel through life phases often unaware that we have come so far and that our bodies have miraculously supported us through the whole gamut. Puberty, pregnancy, childbirth and wise mother, nurturer, seeker, sage, elder ... we flow perfectly well through these without a *How To* manual to hone in on and swat as bedtime reading.

Metaphysically, we know that everything happens from within and works its way through to its outer manifestation, from cause to effect, and our bodies are the outer, reflected effect of what's going on in there. What is less appreciated is that within us are our thoughts, beliefs, emotions, words and deeds; this is our inner world and our body is the outer mirror. When our body shows us that something is not quite right we often look in the wrong place. For example, I have a pounding headache, so do I take a headache pill and ignore the cause; or do I look at what's going on around me and at my life to see where the blocks are and what I can release in thought? We may do both of these or neither. The thing is, firstly, to realise that our body is one huge reflective mirror of our inner lives. We live in the outcome of our thoughts and beliefs and so we can look at our bodies as an opportunity to explore within and heal more deeply, getting to the core and heart of the issue through the mind. Look to your body as a messenger and LISTEN carefully to what's going on in it, the answers are always there. We are so much more powerful than we ever imagine and this power is the power of who we are.

Back when Louise Hay wrote *You Can Heal Your Life*, bringing the mind body connection into wider consciousness, she was stating what has been known for aeons; now, scientists are proving this phenomenon in empirical ways but it's nothing new! A connected mind and body is who we are as spiritual beings in human existence, but our small, finite minds assume we are powerless to master ourselves. How wrong can we be? Fix the tap, rewire your thoughts and heal from within.

Heart of the lotus mandala

The Quest, The Vision, The Centre

Yvonne Skelly

I FIND MYSELF ON MY BATHROOM FLOOR, January 1994, aged seventeen. I am overcome with emotion, I howl out cries, curling myself in a foetal position on the floor. These cries come from some empty, lonely chasm within my being, that until now I did not know even existed. I am not even sure I recognise the sounds coming from my apparently broken soul. Is it even me making these incoherent sobs? I feel a deep sadness, frustration and unease erupting from the very centre of my being, forcing its way out through these frantic cries and sobs, demanding my attention. I implore to the heavens, hands clasped in prayer and ask myself, the universe, God, whoever will listen... why I am feeling this way? This does not make sense.

I am half way through my first year at the prestigious University College, Dublin. I have done my parents very proud. I was one of the first in my extended family to attend university. My parents, both from working class backgrounds, were themselves deprived of the opportunity to finish secondary school, never mind go to college, due to lack of finances, and burdened from a young age with the responsibility to earn money for their family's survival. My mother swore she would do everything she could to ensure I and my sister did not have the same fate. She wanted to ensure we would give ourselves the best possible chance of succeeding in life, of being strong independent women, without having to depend on anyone else for a good standard of living. A good education could make this possible. She has, to her credit, kept her promise, even if financially it was yet another burden on her and my father.

So, there I am studying for a Bachelor of Science degree and have settled in well. I've made loads of new friends and am fully embracing the social side of college life. Freshers' week, partying, socialising – you name it, I'm there. Life is busy, exciting, fun, lively, good – or so I think. Perhaps I should mention, that whilst, yes, the social side is amazing, the study part is uninspiring, I simply don't enjoy it. It doesn't excite me. It's dull and uninteresting on every level. I am failing exams and assignments, which to be fair, reflect the interest and effort I'm applying to my academics.

Crouched on my knees and hands clasped in desperation, seeking guidance, I beg, glancing up for inspiration, clarity, anything... why do I feel this way? I wait for an answer. Nothing comes. I lie down on the bathroom floor again and continue to sob, eventually crying myself into a silent lull. In sleep I find stillness and appease my tormented soul. Time passes; I awake, still in foetal position, on the cold tiles of the bathroom floor and slowly become aware of my surroundings, with memories emerging of my predicament before I fell asleep. I still feel fragile, somewhat weak, but I have clarity. Oh my God, I have clarity! Have my prayers been answered?

I know what I need to do – for me, for my soul, for my own journey; but I'm not sure it is going to meet with approval. I breathe deeply. I need to follow through on my actions, regardless of the reactions of others. I must honour my own intuitive knowing. I can feel courage rising within, filling up the empty chasm that revealed itself so ferociously before – now, I am ready to take the next steps. Quit College. Well, quit science; it's not for me – I have zero interest. I shan't waste my precious time and energy on something I find boring. I'll return to do a new course. Social science, that's more me! Life and people fascinate me. Now that's a course I could embrace, enjoy and feel inspired by.

As predicted, my parents are shocked, disappointed and thinking despairingly of the several thousand pounds wasted on nothing. Perhaps they're worried I'll become a college drop-out and never return, become a 'failure' in my mother's aspirations for me to be a strong independent woman. I vow to find a job whilst waiting for my new course, and work in the local pub full-time, saving money and paying back the wasted fees. My new friends are shocked too, but I don't care because the relief I feel in every cell of my body is palpable. My meltdown was a wake-up call. It was my soul demanding attention, asking me to be truthful with myself, my values, my authentic divine essence. It was ultimately a gift and I'm so glad I listened to and honoured this gift.

On a side note, during the time between dropping out and starting anew, I met the love of my life at the pub. He was, and continues to be, a huge part of my life and journey. So, yes, my life path was ebbing and flowing nicely again, bringing into existence those who were to become an integral part of it.

What if I had not had the conviction to listen to, recognise and follow my intuitive knowing – what if I had ignored my soul's cries?

The Quest

It's September 1996, and I sit alone on the bottom stair; through dampened eyes, I stare blankly at a newly opened pack of cigarettes. I resign myself to the fact that I won't be finishing this pack of cigarettes any time soon and decide to gift them to my friend. At the tender age of twenty, I have just found out that I am to be a mother. Me? A Mother? I sigh. I can't remember even having held a baby, so how in God's name am I going to be able to raise one? My emotions are mixed; I fleet between polarities of joy at creating a life form with a boyfriend I love with all my heart, to shock, distress and increasing unease at how my family, friends and wider social community are going to react to this news. I also feel a profound and everlasting well of pure love deep within my being for this embryo, growing inside, that I have co-created with the man who captured my heart two years before. My timing, of course, is impeccable! I am in my final year studying social science, and my due date is to be slap bang in the middle of my final exams! Nine months pregnant doing finals for an honours degree, I do love a challenge!

As I try to gather my thoughts and the snot and tears that overwhelm me, I gaze again at the now discarded pack of cigarettes. I realise that I already have an incredible desire to nurture and protect this tiny soul in my womb, so smoking is definitely not an option, no matter what! As I ponder further, it dawns on me that smoking wasn't an issue when it was just *me* in the equation. It is okay to sabotage my own well-being through this toxic addiction, but not my baby. Why? Why is that so?

Was my baby more worthy of respect, love and care than I was? The answer seems obvious. Of course not! We all deserve love and respect, including me, and yet, my actions suggested otherwise. This tiny observation triggered a deepening of my journey into self-love, healing and spiritual understandings. A spiritual quest if you will, but where would this journey bring me?

The Mother

My experiences of motherhood were not always easy; I was young and had to teach myself everything about babies. I genuinely did not know that babies need special formula milk (I kid you not, I learnt about that in the biology section of UCD library, whilst I was studying and very pregnant)! Like most new mothers, I felt physically overwhelmed by the demands of this tiny human. To compound the physical exhaustion, I worked in a bar at night and would come home late to be woken early by my daughter as early morning alarm clock. I was often emotionally and mentally overwhelmed by the responsibility of being a mother. I was young and watched forlornly, as my friends travelled the globe, partied and led what seemed to be carefree, exciting and adventurous lives while I was knee-deep in nappies, washing, mortgage, bills and plans of marriage. As a mother I was worlds apart from my peers. I had a new identity now, one that I had never even considered as part of my life, the enormous responsibility of caring for and rearing this beautiful child.

I had an inner conflict: loving my child with every cell but another part of me feeling deprived of expressing my self or living my youth to the maximum; it felt whipped away from me. With that came guilt, the shame of even thinking this way having been blessed with a healthy baby, a supportive partner who adored us both and a family network who were understanding and caring in their love for the first grandchild.

The Healing

October 2000 and I'm four months pregnant with my second child. I see an advertisement for something called Reiki, some kind of energy therapy, a two day course. I have no idea what it is, never heard of it, but feel instantly drawn to it. The fact I've even seen the tiny advert in the corner of the shopping centre is quite bizarre, so I book in. Apparently I am the only one who booked in to be attuned to Reiki without having experienced a treatment or knowing what it was! Yet, I feel such familiarity with this energy healing, it makes perfect sense and resonates with what I've read about holistic healing.

This formal introduction to energy healing kick-started a journey of exploration, self-healing and spiritual understanding.

I spent the next few years working on myself and healing wounds from the past: feelings of guilt, shame and pain from lifetimes of experiences that revealed themselves when the time was right. My journey was long, often hard and not for the faint hearted, but it was a necessary one, and mostly a joyful one too, despite the challenges. It removed every barrier, allowing my true essence to emerge, where pure love, joy and fulfilment reside. Over the next few years, I learnt many other healing modalities, each one an essential part of my journey towards self love and empowerment.

What if I had not seen that advertisement for Reiki? What if I had ignored that familiar feeling I get when something is important, even if I do not understand why or how it is or will be?

Inspiring Youth

It is now November 2006. I am working full time with a pharmaceutical company. It is a wonderful company to work for, good salary, health benefits, great career prospects. However, at a soul level I feel uninspired. I am not meant for this type of corporate, profit driven at all costs, work. I am more of a social science girl!

A non profit education charity come into our office to explain about volunteering opportunities working with local youth, encouraging them to remain in education and learn more about the world of work and the vast array of career opportunities available, basically inspiring our youth to reach their potential. I volunteer to deliver a programme over a number of weeks in a local disadvantaged school (with some trepidation!) I feel nervous at the thought of teaching nine to ten-year-old children, but take a deep breath and decide to go for it. It is a topic close to my heart as I know how education opens so many doors in people's lives.

I completed the required training and got chatting to the charity's trainer about her job and what she did. I shared with her that her job sounded exactly like the type of work I yearned for. Something that was socially conscious, giving back, meaningful. It turned out they were looking for staff and by the time I had finished delivering my programme for the charity, yours truly was their newest team member!

I had to take a pay cut and lost my corporate job benefits such as a lucrative pension and health care for my family, but it did not matter to me. Doing something fulfilling was my objective and so began another phase in my career. I ended up being promoted within six months, with a pay increase to boot!

I have not once regretted that decision to change and still, ten years later, work part time for this organisation recruiting, training and supporting business volunteers to deliver programmes in schools, inspiring local youth. I also have the pleasure of working directly with some children on a range of programmes and projects that aim to develop their potential and build their confidence. It is a rewarding job as I see both volunteers and students getting a lot from their experiences. I meet interesting and wonderful students and volunteers both in the companies I liaise with and in the schools.

What if I had not followed my heart and chosen instead to stay with the better paying job with more career prospects? Sure, I would have more money and 'benefits' now, but would I have the same sense of fulfilment? Sometimes, we take an apparent loss but, in doing so, gain in ways beyond our comprehension.

No Comparisons

My spiritual quest for knowledge and understanding has led me to realise that comparing my life experiences, or lack of them, to others is a futile waste of energy. We are spiritual beings having a human experience; comparing my life to someone else's does not make any sense in the grand picture, yet I fell into that trap so many times. I compared my life to that of my friends, family or even celebrities. What a waste of precious energies. On a soul level I believe I chose to incarnate in this body in order to experience certain life events, so what may seem unfair or unpleasant from my human perspective, is the perfect divine soul experience for my highest growth. Comparing myself to others from a better or worse perspective is a pointless exercise; everyone is in the perfect time and place for their unique soul expression on their journey. When I shift my perspective from human to soul level, the view changes dramatically. There is no longer a need to compare, to compete. What's left is co-operation, collaboration, a sense of connectedness and purpose.

Solfeggio

Summer 2011. Fresh off the back of studying two intensive (and expensive!) modules in cranio-sacral therapy, I find myself browsing the internet in my never ending quest for more knowledge on self-empowerment and healing. I come across articles about sacred sounds called *solfeggio* frequencies which immediately grab my attention – something within me feels a sense of familiarity about them. I'm keen to learn more about these sacred tones.

To my dismay, there's no-one in Ireland who trains people how to use these tones as a healing modality so I purchase a home-study pack from the States. I'm intrigued about the potential in these healing sounds and look into courses to qualify myself as a practitioner, but they are all hosted in America. Maybe I could go to the States? But, a few phone calls and calculations later, I realise that financially that's not an option right now. I call the centre in the hope that perhaps there are courses running in Ireland or even Europe? No. But they kindly send me the name of a teacher on the East side of America who may be slightly cheaper than the West side. I reach out anyway but with decreasing hope and knowing I still can't afford to attend.

Contact is made! It turns out that Susan, the teacher, is also a transatlantic pilot and more than happy to stay over in

Ireland to run some courses. I sit down in awe and smile to myself, what are the chances of this? How many holistic teachers turn out to be pilots in their day jobs? More amazing news is that the flights don't cost her much (just tax and insurance), so we can bring her to Ireland for very little, meaning that the financials are starting to look more optimistic. It has become a viable possibility. Dates are set for a *Solfeggio* body tuner course, plus levels 1 and 2. I really am going to train on how to use sacred tones for healing. And so begins my journey into using sacred tones in my healing practice.

WOW, I am truly humbled and in awe about how the universe aspires to help you when it is part of your path.

Divine Intervention on Line One

Skip on to March 2014, and I'm working part-time for a non-profit education charity. Over the past years I've had many healing and soul-searching adventures. I have discovered and studied different healing modalities, read varied perspectives on living, our purpose here on earth and about spirituality and empowerment. I've continued to venture into the darkest recesses of my soul as I discover, probe and explore. I've experienced overwhelming painful emotions, re-lived and healed traumas from this and past lives. Equally I've felt incredible joy, laughter and fulfilment as I began to rediscover the magnificence of who I am – who we all are! I guess you could say I'm at a point in my life where my desire to heal and help humanity has deepened and expanded. I yearn to do it more and more, but despite my heartfelt desire to practise healing as more than a part-time offering, the reality of it increasing to fill my life feels slow to unfold.

Anyway, here I am, patiently waiting in a business reception for a 2 o'clock meeting. My mobile rings and although I wouldn't normally respond to the phone this close to an appointment, I feel the urge to answer. A guy called Olivier is on the end of the phone, querying the possibility of renting rooms in a holistic centre where I no longer work. I explain that I may not be of much assistance, however something within me wants to help this guy out. Perhaps it was his soft French accent with the Irish twang; whatever it was, I promise to pass on his message to the current owner with a view to him renting rooms. We bid our farewells and end the call perfectly in time before my host arrives for the meeting. As promised I follow up two days later and text Olivier information about the rooms. It turns out that the room rental was a non-event; in the grand picture, the call was really an opportunity for us to connect. The cosmos set the wheels in motion.

What if I hadn't answered that phone call? What if I had ignored that inner pull to take the call despite my imminent meeting? This phone call was about to transform my life in ways beyond my imagination or wildest dreams. Not answering it would have created a whole different reality. But answer it I did!

The Group Gathering

Facebook next, and an intriguing invitation to a group healing session in Naas, Ireland, run by Olivier (who has to be the most Irish looking French guy I have ever encountered – Facebook gives a lot away!) and his holistic business partner Darren.

At the time, I was going through a spell of crushing anxiety and fear about mixing at social gatherings, which meant, more often than not, that I allowed the fear to consume me and just stayed at home. Thoughts of a group healing session sent anxieties and fears cascading throughout my body, I could feel my tummy doing somersaults. Anyway, I always practised extreme discernment about who and where I went for healing as a lot of healers didn't resonate with my own experiences or inner knowings and I just did not connect with them in a heartfelt way. But, in my heart, I knew it was very important for me to go to this particular healing session, so I took a deep breath and accepted the invitation, putting massive trust in the universe. It was squeaky bum time, a lesson in trust and surrender...

D Day arrives for the group healing session, I am feeling a mixture of nervousness, fear and sheer excitement; terrified but so looking forward this gathering. I affirm with the universe that no matter what happens, it's all for the greater good (even if I have an anxiety meltdown!) and decide I shall go with an open mind and heart, breathe deeply and just let things flow. As it is, I am one of the first to arrive. I instantly feel at home meeting Darren and Olivier; I feel a sense of joy and playfulness, and know I have made the right decision to come. I start to relax and breathe with slightly more ease.

We do some chanting to start off proceedings, and then move into a quiet meditation with Darren and Olivier creating the common healing space. I fairly quickly go off into a vision.

The Vision

A brilliant white light comes towards my crown and third eye and six majestic beings appear, surrounding my earthly body. They emanate pure love and bliss, they are captivating and somehow familiar to me. They lovingly explain that they know how frustrated I am. Indeed, I had long had a sense of a specific job of healing to do this lifetime, so 'frustrated' was an understatement, I just wanted to get on with my path and yet I felt stagnated, frozen in fear and anxiety, unable to see how this was to happen. They explained that I did have a very important job to do and soon the timing would be right. In fabulous divine tones, they declared, 'Dearest child, be patient, your time is near.'

PAUSE! Okay, hello? What you talking about? Important job to do? Eh, Deepak, Eckhart – I think your guides are on the phone for you!

WOW! It was all so loving, warm – blissful. I was on a high, my body floating like a feather, so light and energised. I was euphoric and, somewhere in my being, I knew their prophecies were right. Ignoring internal doubts of whether I was worthy of any important work, I decided to just surrender to the process. If this was to be true, then surely things would begin to happen! I affirmed each morning on my commute to work... 'Oh, dearest ones,' I figured I should reciprocate their grand language when addressing them, 'I offer myself up to serve humanity. Please provide opportunities for me to do it in the best way possible with love, peace, joy, truth, playfulness and laughter.'

And so began the next part of my adventure or, perhaps, my important work?

The Centre

Now it's September 2014. Out of the blue, I am offered the opportunity to go into business with Olivier Florian. Yes, the same guy from the random phone call, group healing and that mad vision from earlier in the year! At best, you could say my association with Olivier was a casual fleeting acquaintance, and yet here I was, ready to go into business with him. We discussed opening a holistic centre, one that we and other therapists could work from. We barely knew each other and I had no financial capital to offer – I was clear about that from the outset, but Olivier just told me to breathe and allow the universe to sort it out – that's another day's story! In fact, I was already struggling financially without the additional burden of a therapy centre to finance and sustain.

We set about opening our holistic centre in Naas, a small town in Ireland which, it should be said, already had three holistic centres. My mind told me I was mad to even consider this, that it was doomed to fail. Even now I smile when reflecting on the situation; on paper it wasn't looking a great opportunity, was it? It looked a massive risk. However, as we talked through the possibility and viewed various premises, my heart *knew* this was okay. It was not going to fail. It was going to be a wonderful adventure. I allowed myself to breathe through any mental niggles that presented themselves and to relax into the intuitive knowing within my heart. I am so so grateful now that I found the courage to allow my heart to supersede my mind.

Imagine, had I not done that?

Today, it's a thriving holistic centre. We have over thirty therapists working here, and people travel from all over Ireland and abroad to attend our workshops or to host workshops themselves. It has been pure joy for me to be involved. Olivier and I have forged a brilliant business partnership and firm friendship, one filled with adventure, joy and playfulness as we embark on our individual soul's journey to reach our own potential and work together, creating somewhere for visitors and therapists to blossom. Every day, I feel blessed and fortunate to have been given this opportunity and humbled to have created this wonderful space for people to learn, grow and heal in. Olivier and I do some healing work together, offering house energy clearings all over Ireland, with incredible results.

The centre offered me a practise space and opportunities to work with, and learn from, gifted spiritual healers and teachers. It has created expansion in every part of my being. In short, it has been a major part of my own spiritual growth. True, there have been times of tremendous challenge within myself as I continue to remove the barriers to realising my own potential. I know from many years of being on the spiritual path that it's all part of the healing and nurturing process – being open and willing to look at the darkest aspects of unresolved issues and pain within.

When I work on a deep soul level, to release and heal past wounds, my energy recalibrates to a different resonance because I grow and expand my true essence. The outward projection of this reflects back to me in my everyday world. It can feel like a breakdown at times, when old dynamics with people and places adjust to new energies, but ultimately it is a break*through* as a more healed self allows the new to come into existence, creating a capacity for more joy, adventure and happiness in my life. Opening the centre has enabled me to bring much more joy into my life. And, just as my heart's knowing had assured me, it has not burdened me financially in any way.

What if I had allowed my head to overrule my heart's knowing, allowed apparent logic to make the decision for me? Sometimes logic does not see the bigger picture. What if I had succumbed to the fear of failure? What if I had allowed my fear of lack to supersede my inner knowing?

The Paris Trip

November 2015 and I am sipping coffee. My emotions are unsettled. I feel a whirlpool of emotions within. I am full of self-doubt, questioning my worthiness, my ability to do this work. What's the point? I am due to fly to Paris that afternoon for a weekend of healing work with Olivier. A few months before, we were so excited to be going to Paris. We decided, on a whim at a holistic business strategy plan meeting, to book the weekend and just allow the universe to flow, bringing whatever healing and clients were needed.

This morning we are due to fly and the excitement is a distant memory. Olivier has bookings for the whole weekend but I have nothing: nada, zip, zilch. I plan to visit some holistic centres and learn more about the holistic world in Paris with a view to future workshops, but beyond that I have no meetings arranged. No clients, no healing sessions, and I'm feeling sorry for myself. Why would anyone book to see me when Olivier, an exceptional healer, is available? Of course, all these feelings of unworthiness, lack of confidence are simply my own stuff! I feel like crying. What use shall I be in Paris? I convince myself I have nothing to offer ☹.

I breathe. I share my thoughts with Olivier, who very simply says it's up to me if I go, that of course he would love me to share the adventure with him but, without judgement or pressure, the choice is mine and mine alone. He will go along with whatever I feel is best for me. I breathe again and hear a very clear and strong voice in my head, 'Go to Paris, when you get there you will fully understand why'. So I take a deep breath and say, 'That's it -– I am going!' I decide my fears and feelings of self-doubt, can take a backseat whilst there, I'll work through them and... off I go!

Paris, beautiful Paris. Now that I am here I am loving being in this city. I am filled with joy and adventure. Whilst Olivier works his busy schedule, I have lots of time to myself. I wander through the streets visiting holistic centres we had identified as of potential interest. I sit and drink coffee outside, thoroughly enjoying the atmosphere and vibrancy of this city. I write, lots. The writing flows.

This evening, Olivier and I visit his friend Martine who has prepared a beautiful meal for us and then we take the metro home about 8.30pm. Life is good, we both feel joyful, blessed to be in Paris doing what we love! Little do we know what is happening above ground as we take the Metro. When we get back to where we are staying (Estelle's, Olivier's friend's apartment), I receive a text from my mother, 'Are you okay?' A bit odd, I think? 'Yes Mom, I'm okay, had a lovely day!' Then more texts, Facebook messages from family, friends and work colleagues asking, 'Are you okay?' 'Where are you?' 'Are you safe?' We had posted on Facebook earlier about our trip to Paris, so I guess a lot of people knew we were there! Okay, this is *really* odd, why is everyone texting us? What's happening? A shooting? What? When?

It is Friday 13th November 2015. We turn on the TV to learn about the siege, shootings, bombings, the absolute carnage that is unfolding in central Paris tonight. It is terrifying to watch. I generally don't watch mainstream TV because it can be very negative and low vibration. It is hard not to feel fearful, tense and incredibly sad as the tragedies and stories unfold before us. But I also begin to understand why I am here, in Paris, this weekend. Is that voice in my head right? What were the chances of us booking a healing weekend in Paris on this weekend of all weekends?

My lack of appointments has given me lots of time. I have recently bought a Brandberg crystal that is great for planetary healing. I've brought it with me so I promise myself that I will make optimum use of my time, walking the streets of central Paris, crystal in tow, to channel in healing energies and intentions everywhere I go. Maybe I am not completely useless after all. At one point I sit on a few steps, overlooking one of the grand boulevards normally, I suspect, vibrant with people but now patrolled by armed police and a few brave souls willing to defy the fear soaked atmosphere and carry on. I sit quietly, observing, with my Brandberg in my hands and allow healing energies to flow through my body. Within the ether, I call upon the assistance of my soul family, healers, angels, guides and any multi-dimensional beings aligned with love, compassion, truth, wisdom, joy, laughter and playfulness. I feel healing energies flow through me. I know it is a drop in the ocean, but every bit helps and I am privileged to offer this as a gesture to the universe, ready to be of service.

After thirty minutes I stand up and look behind me. I am on the steps of the Musical Museum. I smile, how funny that I sit here; I work with sacred sound in my healing practice so the synchronicity is not wasted on me and I rejoice at the universe's nod to sound!

Oh, how humbling that I am here in Paris this weekend, to be able to do something positive, something worthwhile. I feel overwhelming gratitude to have this opportunity. Olivier, in his own way, is doing the same as he works with his clients over the weekend, channelling in healing energy. He too, despite all the chaos of that weekend, experiences pure love, joy and healing as he works. Is this the reason I have been guided so clearly to go? I walk the legs off myself around central Paris, with love in my heart, transmitting as high vibrational energies as I can, consciously working to transmute the horrific energies that have been unleashed in the city – the energies of pure love, joy and gratitude are the exact energies to transmute those negative imprints created by the carnage.

Truly, I felt blessed to be there to play a teeny part in helping to heal this wonderful city. Again, I was thankful I had allowed myself to be guided by my heart and not held back by my fears or feelings of self-doubt and unworthiness. There is always a bigger picture at play!

Divine Feminine Empowerment

July 2016. As I write this I am forty years old and the journey continues. My healing work now involves an eclectic mix of all I have learnt and continue to learn – as Socrates once said: true wisdom is knowing how little you know.

I am expanding my healing work into running group workshops, mainly for women. They are intuitively guided and their topics vary. I am drawn more and more to work with empowering the divine feminine in myself and, by extension, with those who participate. As I work with groups, I gain more understanding of how I, other women and indeed society in general carry the wounds of a deeply oppressed and wounded divine feminine expression. I witness many women, myself very much included, carrying deep wounds, from experiences in their own lives or from experiences within their ancestral lines: the collective hurt of unresolved pain from the oppression of divine feminine energies. Yes, even mainstream science now confirms that ancestral trauma can be carried through many generations in our DNA. These wounds manifest as self-sabotage, lack of self-confidence, feeling unworthy or powerless, angry or frustrated and feeling unheard or unacknowledged. Wounds within the divine feminine are equally damaging to men, so it's not just about women. We are all in this together, as one heals, so the other heals – we are all one at the end of the day ☺

Divine feminine attributes of wisdom, love, compassion, truth and intuitive knowing, these are the attributes that, when brought to the forefront and in perfect alignment with the divine masculine, can move mountains and create miracles. I am blessed to witness women who release and transcend these wounds and I see them come into their power, tentatively with grace. It is a beautiful sight to behold. It is inspiring, humbling and quite simply transformational. The world needs more of this!

How does one go about beginning to heal the wounds and pain within, to nurture oneself and start to live an empowered, joyful, authentic and fulfilling life?

Where to begin?

I can only share what I experience, how I work towards realising my own potential by healing and nurturing myself. I am on a continuous journey and will be until my time on earth ends. A good starting place is to realise that I have everything I need within to create a fulfilling, joyful and happy life. I don't need any guru or outside person to fix my life; I can do that. I have the power. I have the choice. I choose.

By all means, I can and do, call upon the assistance of other people's experiences, skills and healing abilities to facilitate my journey. When I do this from a heart centred place, from the intuitive knowing within, I am living in a self-directed, empowered way. When living from this space of inner knowing, I experience magical synchronicities whereby perfect teachers, healers, circumstances and events manifest, ones that are best for me at that moment. My life is littered with shining examples: college, Reiki, Solfeggio, the Centre, Paris…

David Icke sums this up nicely in his book *Remember Who You Are (2012)*, when he says:

> *'I roll my eyes when I hear these long drawn out explanations by gurus of every kind telling people to do this, that and the other to become 'enlightened'. We ARE enlightened, it is our natural state…'*

So, how do I connect with this intuitive knowing within, this heart-centred place? Well, first off, I breathe. And then I breathe again! And breathe again!!

The Breath

Most of us live busy lives, an endless cycle of work, housework, looking after children or family, daily tasks and responsibilities. Society, as it is currently structured, doesn't lend itself well to allowing time and space to just sit, breathe and be. Society often projects a perception that sitting and doing nothing, as in *just being*, is lazy or unproductive, a social taboo; but it is such a powerful way to connect consciously with your essence and ultimately to the powerhouse of all that you are and can create. So, I ignore that group thinking and I give myself permission to find time, even if just for two minutes a day. I relax, breathe and am still. I don't need to sit in the lotus position on a mountain top to connect within. Sure, that might be wonderful and, no doubt, a truly awesome experience! But I don't make things complicated.

I can do it anywhere, anytime – even on my commute to work, in my lunch break, when my kids are out and about. When I set the intention, I find the time! There is always time somewhere in your day to check in with your heart space and inner knowing. You just need to set the intention - *the intention to connect within.* Allow me to share with you one of my favourite mini-meditations:

Heart Meditation

- ♥ Breathe gently with focus. Breathe in a long slow inhalation; breathe out a long slow exhalation. Visualise your feet connecting with the earth.
- ♥ Visualise golden roots coming from your toes, heels and ankles, connecting you to the sacred energies of Mother Earth, anchoring you firmly. Feel yourself becoming centred, grounded. Allow your mind to become still and focus your attention on your heart space. Just breathe in and out softly, without effort.
- ♥ Visualise a tiny glow of gold and white light in your heart space. This glow is a spark of divine light, pure love manifest.
- ♥ See the spark of love growing and expanding from your heart space as you continue to inhale and exhale in a rhythmic ebb and flow. See its glow of pure love manifest, this glow of compassion, wisdom, playfulness, truth, joy and laughter as it expands beyond your physical body, beyond the room. The expansion is limitless.

- ♥ If you seek guidance on a person, place or thing, then visualise that person or situation being immersed in this blissful expansion of love from your heart. Allow yourself to experience the stillness in your heart within this space, the awareness of your purist divine essence – it's the place of all possibility, of all knowing.
- ♥ Remember, the mind thinks, the heart KNOWS.

Within stillness
Silence Speaks only Truth
Only Love is Real
Of all Possibility
All that is, was and ever shall be

This very simple exercise, or intention, can have profound effects on your life. Living your life from the heart centred perspective is life changing. It can transform your life beyond recognition. Each and every one of us has, within, all the knowledge needed. By all means let others be a source of knowledge or a beacon to show a way, but ultimately you are your own guru. The tricky part is about removing lifetimes of programming that prevents us connecting to the infinite source of truth and knowledge within; then being brave enough to actually carve out the path as it shows itself, to face your fears head on and go for it! Once you engage with this knowledge, and embrace the power you hold within, life promises to present itself with amazing opportunities and experiences.

Womb Wisdom Meditation

This next meditation is for connecting with, healing and balancing your *womb wisdom* – that space of divine feminine essence, a place of inner knowing, purity of compassion and love, that divine creative force capable of all possibility. Allow at least twenty minutes for this meditation, making yourself comfortable in a space you'll be undisturbed. You could read this aloud to yourself just before going to sleep or another idea is to read it in a group with other women.

♥ Breathe gently with focus. Breathe in a long slow inhalation; breathe out a long slow exhalation. Visualise your feet connecting with the earth below. Visualise golden roots coming from your toes, heels and ankles connecting you to the sacred energies of Mother Earth, anchoring you firmly. Feel yourself becoming centred, grounded. See these golden roots expanding outwards and downwards, like a vast network of roots, like the mighty oak tree. See these roots going right into the very centre of Mother Earth, connecting with her great heart, compassion and sacred wisdom. Visualise the golden roots mixing with the energies of the core of the earth.

- Now visualise these sacred motherly earth energies, filled with love, wisdom and compassion, mixing with and expanding up into your vast network of golden roots, nourishing, cleansing and clearing as they go. See the golden roots mixing with magenta pink energies of the earth as they travel upwards, reaching your toes, feet, ankles. Slowly visualise golden energy mixed with magenta pink as it expands further through your physical body, working its way up your calves, thighs, hips, your internal organs, spine, shoulders, arms, hands, head until your entire body is engulfed with healing energy. This energy cleanses, clears and rebalances your physical body, permeating every cell, every DNA strand, ever expanding, and radiating throughout until your entire mental, emotional and spiritual bodies radiate gold and magenta pink healing energies across all timelines and existence.
- In this state of pure love, bliss and joy, call upon the sacred healing energies of Holy Grandmother Anna, Mother Mary, Mary Magdalene and Yeshua. Call on all multidimensional

beings, your guides, teachers and angels who are aligned with love, peace, joy, compassion, wisdom, truth, laughter and playfulness.

- Visualise yourself surrounded by these beings of light in a loving bubble of healing energies and see them connecting with your sacral chakra. Focus your attention on this area and allow the healing energies to work their magic.
- Ask for all wounds deep within your sacred womb and sacred divine feminine to be released, healed and balanced for your highest good, and for all those with whom you are connected.
- Surrender to any emotions you may be feeling, allow yourself to release and let go, immersing yourself in energies of pure love and compassion, seen as glowing gold, white and platinum healing energies. Allow yourself to rest in this space of healing for a few moments, or for as long as feels right for you…
- Visualise a situation, person, place or thing that you would like to heal or manifest in your life. See this situation being lovingly healed, nurtured and created by the divine creative healing force within your sacred womb centre. See it, feel it, sense it, know it.
- When you are ready, bring your attention back to your breath. Observe your self breathing in and out effortlessly. Bring your awareness, slowly and gently back into your body, allowing

awareness to travel from your toes, upwards through your whole body, until you are fully present and aware of your physical surroundings.

- Take a few deep breaths before completing your meditation. If you feel called to, journal any messages, visions or insights gained during the meditation. Offer gratitude.

Heart really is where it's at!

Mainstream science is beginning to discover the importance of the heart centre and its significance in the grand picture of our mental, emotional and physical health. The Institute of HeartMath, in the United States, is a non-profit, education and research organisation who 'research and develop reliable, scientifically based tools that bridge the connection between heart and mind and deepen people's connection with the hearts of others' (www.heartmath.org). What they have discovered is that the heart has a powerful electromagnetic field, more powerful than the brain and it has its own intelligence; more neurons travel from the heart to the brain than vice versa. They have also discovered that when the heart is in harmony and *coherence* with the brain, that this translates into a far more expanded awareness in the individual.

Heart, through its powerful electromagnetic field, expands further when in coherence: when a person is in a blissful state or is experiencing positive emotions such as love, joy, laughter, appreciation and so on, it impacts on their body and indeed their environment. Remember, *mind thinks, heart knows*. Heart is aware of oneness, of connectedness and therefore has far more capacity to give and receive compassion, love, wisdom, joy and innate truth.

On a similar note, there have been many studies on the impact of meditation (or what I would term heart consciousness) on the wider social community, which backs up the idea that states of happiness, joy, appreciation can impact not only on you, but on the world around you. Studies in the US have shown that when fifteen minutes of meditation was introduced in secondary school, pupils began to perform better, behave better, attendance was up and violence was down. It was transformational to the school's environment.

It might seem like a very simple idea, but connecting with your *heart space* is a great place to start. It is the key to understanding yourself and your own journey; no-one knows better than you. You know within yourself the best way to heal and nurture yourself. It will lead you to the right people, places, opportunities for your highest good which are tailor made for your unique path. You have the power, the choice, and the ability to create.

Empowering, isn't it?

Unicorn mandala

Unconditional Self Love

Laura

I AM COMPELLED TO WRITE ABOUT SELF LOVE NOW as I believe it's the key to it all. It's taken me so long to get to grips with what loving myself really means and I have to share it with you. For me, self love means having no judgment on myself about whatever is happening around me. It means knowing that I am enough because I am the great power of life and it also means being willing to accept that, in all that happens, I am doing the best I can and I am always guided and loved for my highest good.

What I have learned, and still am learning, is that:

- Self love is my right and it is always SELF-FULFILLING.
- Self love is an act of self-fullness and, as we willingly open our hearts to loving ourselves, we see our world shift, re-organise and change in the most surprising ways.
- Self love allows us to create life as we dream and deserve it to be as we open to sharing this love and healing energy with those we love, with our communities and the world.
- Self love sets us on a clear pathway to understanding and knowing who we are and what makes us feel good in life.
- Self love gives us real inner power to make loving and caring choices for our lives, to draw lines, to live in our truth, and to define our YES and our NO, not because we have to, because we *want* to.

Many think of self love as an unnecessary, selfish indulgence or even shameful. *Who does she think she is?* comes to my mind here or, *I must put others before me to be accepted and liked,* or at the other extreme, *If they're happy then I am happy*. Such statements position us far away from living or loving our inner power. The choice to love ourselves fully is electing to live in our realness, our authentic selves and in our true power whatever is going on around us, with no guilt, shame, shoulds or oughts in our minds. It's a choice to turn within at moments of madness and say instead, *I am doing the best I can and I love myself for that!*

Society is driven by image and external influence, social media, press, quick-fix language. All these are part of life's collective consciousness that exists around us and which can emanate messages of fear into our lives and the world we live in. Again we have a choice, we can willingly choose to accept it all… or not. We don't have TV in our home and this is our conscious choice to not be bombarded with automatic messaging that comes from a place of fear or 'not good enough'. Yes, there's also great TV and we pick it up on the tablet as and when we feel to. It's just good knowing we can take charge of our own living space and environment and we consciously choose to do that. Our children are sucked into the media like magnets. The number of times I dream of just grabbing and catapulting my daughter's phone into the stratosphere as I realise the images, messaging and indoctrination looming in the virtual world and way beyond parents' control to monitor or ban! Of course I also realise there is nothing that we can control other than our own thoughts and feelings, but by doing this much, taking charge and mastering the art of self love and acceptance, we send out an enlightening ripple from our centre to the rest of the world – our children cannot sidestep that ripple!

Self Love Check List

Answer *Yes, No* or *Sometimes* to the questions below in quick time, jotting down your first natural feeling as your response. This is your truth. Revisit here in three and six weeks, after you've put the self love exercises in place.

- ♥ Do you feel good about yourself?
- ♥ Are you taking time daily to go within, meditate and journal?
- ♥ Are you comfortable saying *No* and meaning it?
- ♥ Do you know and live by your values?
- ♥ Do you trust life, do you believe in yourself?
- ♥ Do you have loving thoughts for yourself?
- ♥ Do you put yourself first – in all ways?
- ♥ Do you feel at peace within?
- ♥ Do you feel love all around you?
- ♥ Are you prepared to take risks for what you believe in?
- ♥ Do you practice forgiveness daily?

- ♥ Are you in pain, physical or emotional?
- ♥ Do you look only to yourself for fulfilment, joy and appreciation?
- ♥ Do you love and accept yourself unconditionally for who you are?

This isn't a test, it is a marker for where you are at the moment – make no judgment. You'll be working on your answers to bring about self love as a natural state of being. It's your empowered journey and one to be taking with POWER in your heart. It's to be enjoyed, so use this list again at any time to gain clarity about where you are with loving yourself.

The choice is ours, we are infinitely powerful as spiritual beings on our human journey and the key is to *know* what we want to experience in this life. For me, it's unconditional love and that's why I am devoted to expanding this awareness in childrens' lives. I believe we are each responsible for bringing this awareness to our children and allowing them to experience the beauty of loving themselves unconditionally. As a child, how many times were you told that you were good enough? Did you receive clear messages of being loved and accepted unconditionally, of being enough? If so, this is reassuring and I hope you are living with the outcome of a stream of loving messages that now support your adult life. Those messages weren't always there for so many, whose parents and teachers simply did not have their own tools of knowing or understanding. If someone is not able or willing to love themselves unconditionally, then how can they teach it to people close to them? Self love means a constant involvement and awareness which demands attention in all ways, not a quick fix that can be shelved once looked at; it calls to be nurtured, contemplated, healed and accepted as a way of life.

Self Love is Your Inner Calling

So, let's get one thing clear, loving yourself is not vanity or narcissism. And it's certainly not about looking in the mirror to criticise or fault what we see, or feeling we need to change things visually to make us look better, be a better person, or improve our life. Unconditional self love is about accepting and lovingly discovering who we are within and living by a set of loving, supportive, healing principles and values that allow us to fully express and accept ourselves just as we are. To put this in place, we must first realise that we are each divinely loved by life and here as an expression of life's love. Self love is a gift and we can live life from our hearts authentically knowing ourselves as we learn to embrace it and expand into the gift. We are taught that if we fix life from the outside things will fall into place and we can then be happy. Truthfully, life works very differently – it's the other way around and, as I wrote previously, we can't control the outside at all, only control our own thoughts, beliefs, feelings, emotions, words, actions. This is self-responsibility and free will and as we align to them we bring on the magic.

We are each blessed with a golden pathway to love, but love can only flow from us if we allow it to flow in and through us. Looking within, meditating and journalling are all part of being fully aware. This is the path of self-discovery that allows us to grow, to be the best that we can be and to live our life fully expanded into love. It takes wanting and willing to make changes, to renew habits and to commit to a deeper knowing that YOU are in charge of you.

Self Love Easily…

- ♥ Enhances your inner confidence and faith.
- ♥ Lets you LIVE in your authentic truth.
- ♥ Aligns you with the POWER within, to know yourself and your heart's desire, so allows you to embrace optimal health.
- ♥ Reflects back unconditional love from outside.
- ♥ Expands feelings of health, joy, abundance and inner peace.
- ♥ Reorganises life and regenerates loving experiences around you.

Each of these effects is truly great and they are natural outcomes that loving yourself can instantly have on your life. The most significant is that loving and accepting ourselves unconditionally makes us feel good about ourselves from deep inside. This one factor can transform the way life treats us. Creating positive experience and feeling good about life attracts more of the same feelings. So feeling *great* opens a gate for more love, healing, joy, abundance, wealth and fulfillment. But be careful, claiming your inner power isn't just about looking good or picking up your confidence for a day or two so that it spills over into your life. It's a solid knowing that whatever's happening you have the inner resources to say, *I love myself unconditionally*. Your path to self love is a journey of growth and wisdom, one to walk in grace for your whole life. Along the way the road may pass places where you don't think you want to be, but STOP right there, because that's where you need to be in order to grow or look deeper within, and you will see opportunities for deeper acceptance, offering you loving and healing self-discovery. Love heals all and each moment gifts a magnificent opportunity to heal within and let that healing produce ripples and waves around us in the outer world.

Looking through the Lens of LOVE

Are you looking at the world through the eyes of love or do you allow built-up feelings of anger, resentment, frustration or fear to lead the way and be your guide? Check in with yourself throughout the day and gauge your essence of self love. The perfect way is to ask yourself...

How Am I Feeling Right Now?

If the feeling is anything other than LOVE then something's gotta give!

In the Love Groove

Feel love in everything you think, feel and *do* and allow this just to be who you are. You will feel the transformation immediately just from doing small things. One heartfelt smile can instantly change how we think and feel. How often do you have meaningful eye contact with a person helping you in a shop? Simply closing your eyes and filling your heart for even ten seconds, with an expansive feeling of love can have a huge impact on your day.

Give Yourself Permission to Shine

Live with unconditional love in your life? You can. It begins here and now with you. This nurturing exercise allows you to connect with the beauty and perfection that you are.

♥ Take five minutes. Close your eyes and connect and ask yourself, *What things do I truly love about myself?* then write them down. You're only looking for good qualities here. Try this exercise daily, creating a big space to see all the beauty that you are. Extend the list and see it as a guide for opening your heart to a constant flow of unconditional love, always with you in every moment. Touch the feelings and connect to the love in your heart for a few minutes, letting your light shine as you realise the beauty of who you truly are within. If things pop up that aren't so supportive let them surface briefly, but now's the time to thank them and let them go... for good.

There's no better way to create change for yourself than to actually practice these steps, however big or small, making them part of your life and there's no better time than NOW. Get ready to give yourself permission to SHINE.

Ruling Your Empire, Mum's the Word

We carry them with love, we bring them in with love,
we bring them up with love – and then they go!

Then there we are, with all that extra time on our hands and just ourselves to focus on. For me, as a lone mum from the word go, it was up to me to pull in all the good emotional feeling I had just to get through the days and be the best I could be for myself and my child. I am so blessed for the emotional support and love that comes through my family which has led to many healings over the years for us all.

Our children's job is to grow, our work is to let go. Having a fourteen-year-old daughter has its 'extra topping' teachings. These extras, however unsavoury I think they are at the time, are always pure gifts – the cherry on the top! Children are here to grow, push, shove, scream and express themselves in their way; it's their job to separate from the mother. Well, you know what our job is? To *let* them go… yikes, that hurts I know! And in the past year I have embraced my power, inner strength, self love, compassion and understanding as I feel the emptiness inside while my daughter does it her way! A child on her own mission to cut the ties of dependence. It's paaiiiiinnnnful to be a bystander, to watch and live through angst and rebellion, and observe our children master the art of growing up. They reflect a different story to us, the story of our ability to grip our own inner power and claim life as we feel we deserve it. Feeling that emptiness within, as I sit in my car at school drop-off, half expecting a kiss goodbye just for old times' sake but instead getting a slammed car door, my heart sinks with a sense of loss because I know that, to grow, our children must energise their being in their own way.

For those of us entering the glorious space of menopause which is a just another state of being, we can choose to transform into a world where we can *rite*fully claim our right of passage into wisdomhood. This might seem a shadow time, but it offers a deep opportunity for inner self-knowing and is a heightened time of pure possibility where you can reclaim your power as a woman and rewrite the script in loving and creative ways. However old or young our children are as we enter this phase it makes no difference, we are always drawn to a sensation that our children are growing away and that can and does have the power to stir up feelings of deep grief with the top thought in our mind being: *And what now? What am I meant to do now she's off having fun and I'm the redundant mother, left holding the tea towel?* Well, this seems like a time of having to reprioritise your life, filling the space that your son or daughter so perfectly filled for so long but, for what it's worth, my take is to simply let go in faith, turning around any feelings of emptiness into discovering a new energy that allows you to embrace creativity and love yourself more deeply. Yes, this time of letting go can also be the perfect chance to get into whatever makes YOU feel good, to prioritise new experiences in your life. Seeking out and embracing things that fully express and fulfill you take you to where you feel filled and valued, energised by life without looking outside, or to your children, for a sense of satisfaction or love. For me, it's creating songs and writing, singing in choirs and, more recently, yoga. I believe that my loving determination to express my voice and create my songs not only gives a strong message to my daughter to live her gifts, it's also showing her that her mum can find fulfilment that doesn't rely on others' approval – and this is another key. It's a waste of time sitting at home worrying and even greater waste to let moments slip by without learning something new. At ages seven, fourteen and twenty-one our bundles of joy tend to push boundaries to the limits, claiming their right to be here in their way, which can be extremely challenging. My daughter began to claim her rights when she was six and has continued ever since... she is a shining light, my greatest teacher and her spirit has guided me to knowing so much including unconditional love, acceptance and true forgiveness.

In the midst of our children's day-to-day growth we may feel as if we are just catching up with their last spurt and then suddenly WHAM they bring on the next thing, so quickly and profoundly that we wonder if they're not just here to grow up but also to get their mums through to the next round of a highly charged bootcamp happening in deep mud! Let them go with love, express yourself creatively and BAM, you have the perfect combo of self-fulfilment and expression, living in faith as well as doing it your way!

It is central to recognise that the belief that our children will make good choices reflects our own faith in the messages and lessons we have shown them before the age of ten. The foundation of our children's choices and actions lie in those thoughts and beliefs we have seeded and the unconditional love and acceptance we have fostered; this is where our faith must stem from, if for nothing else for our own sanity! As my daughter was growing up I would regularly do mirror work with her, planting seeds of love by teaching her to look into the mirror and say the words *I love you* to herself. She did this over and over for days, weeks, months and I am blessed that I showed her this knowing. Now it's a different story and the make-up bag rules any issues of getting the foundation right, yet I feel secure that the seeds are planted and subconsciously she knows that she *is* love, which is what matters. As she grows, this knowing can only strengthen and surface in all its beauty. It's never too late to teach this message to your children, however old or young they are, as when they see you pick up a mirror and say out loud *I love myself just as I am*, they understand loud and clear that you are acknowledging and fulfiling your very own amazingness.

I am so grateful to my deep learning of motherhood and realise that being consistent with my boundaries and knowing where I draw the line is vital for a sense of self-worth in my relationship with my daughter. There are times when I know it is crucial to stay in my truth with my feelings about her choices and making this clear to her, even as she chooses to ignore me, gives me connection with my inner power to stand by that truth. Knowing my *yes* and my *no* is a central part of knowing myself and by clearly stating this, regardless of how it is accepted, is an empowering act. As our children grow and discover their world in their way, they will also live it in their own way, but being strong as a mum is not about shouting or screaming the house down, it's about staying firmly with my loving beliefs. Practice the exercise of speaking your truth and just lettting it go, we can only control our own thoughts and actions.

Loving Kindness

Being kind to yourself is crucial for moment to moment inner peace and one thing I have learned along the way is how vital it is to embrace a loving, supportive network of women who will nurture me if I feel overwhelmed or unsure of life. Of course, all that we are, the strength, power and certainty we relish, comes from deep in our hearts, but there are always moments when a loving friend, a listening ear, a hug from the heart can inspire us to come back to a point of peace and love. Choose your friends and support system with love and care and do ask for help when you need to. This is fundamental to our wellbeing as we so often feel led by a false pressure to achieve everything alone; it is important to embrace asking for support, because you will receive what you need.

It's not always easy to fathom others' choices, especially those close to us, and yet the people who we choose to place in our lives are our biggest teachers. We won't always like or agree with their decisions and we may struggle with situations that are brought straight to our door, yet we can learn so much about ourselves through how we respond to life circumstances. Our children teach us too and our hidden fears are often highlighted by their choices so that emotions run high in our relationship with them. Family life demands that we upgrade our awareness of the effects of alcohol, drugs and sex that are so vividly exposed to all of us online and in the media. Our children are influenced by this exposure, which becomes scary for them and us, especially when these areas become their grown up playground.

Learning ways to willingly step back and take a full breath are essential for clarity, self-care and emotional wellbeing. It can seem frightening when children and those you love become exposed to these lower vibrations of life. If this is your situation, I invite you to affirm that you are doing the very best that you can in all ways; instantly remove any thoughts or feelings of guilt, judgement or blame. Be there for yourself and love yourself first, allowing in friends who can lovingly support you during times of question.

Know that you are never alone, you are always loved.

Yin yang mandala

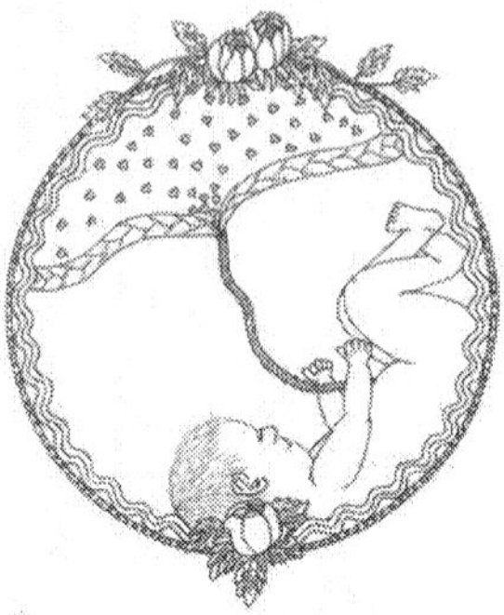

Unleash Your Inner Child

Kate Bartram Brown

A FEW YEARS AGO I WOULD HAVE TURNED OVER THE PAGE if someone had presented me with a book on inner child work. I really had no concept of what this even meant, let alone the effect that our inner child has on our daily life, decisions, success and happiness. However, what I have now seen through my own direct experiences and watching thousands of women's experience, is the sheer joy it brings when we are able to reach that inner child and let them out to play!

The effects of this phenomenon are transformative, yet so simple that many women have managed to change old, limiting habits that have shaped their entire adult lives simply by using a few easy, super-enjoyable techniques each day to allow our all too often forgotten inner child to aid our daily success and happiness.

I want to share with you some ideas that have helped me, and those other women, so that you can bring your own inner child into your daily routine and engage with her. Encouraging your inner child to be involved in your life will have a positive influence, replacing experiences that you might carry from this complex aspect of yourself.

First of all, let me share my experience; only in brief, because I want this to be about you and *your* inner child. I also want you to be able to connect with any children in your life from their level and see the positive effects that you can share with them which, in turn, will help you have a happy day!

The word perfect, it's a funny word; I don't mean ha-ha funny, but its meaning. Some see it as affirmative, others see it as a goal, but the effect of trying to attain and maintain our perception of this word is something that has baffled me my entire life. That word has been my block, my anchor, my hindrance, my catalyst, my entire life. It has shaped life in good ways and bad. It is a word that my inner child discerns, judges and reacts to in every situation I am presented with. If I had understood this in my teens and twenties, well let's just say I would have had a much smoother experience. Now in my late thirties, approaching forty, I'm finally getting it. Ah, wisdom at last... well, at least one can hope!

That word, perfect, has stuck to me since I was a small child and was used to judge my success but, as we know, nothing stays perfect, everything is always changing, as it should be. So my view of success was taken from me by this word, I could always do better, try harder, be prettier, slimmer, smarter, funnier... the list goes on.

Why I created this perception, where it came from, whether it was real, doesn't really matter because that early programming affected me into my adulthood. I felt, and still feel, it's real so knowing where it came from isn't really going to help. Can I change it? Well yes! This is of extreme importance and brings me to my goal in this chapter.

I have learned that the inner child, when ignored, can create as much havoc in our life as a toddler having a meltdown in the supermarket. That is just like what happens inside us when our inner child is ignored, but we often don't give it a second glance.

So, let's look at that again: we don't give it a second glance when it's crying out for attention.

I invite you to close your eyes for a moment

- ♥ Imagine what a small child would feel like if it was ignored and rejected again and again. In fact, let's now imagine how you feel if you see a child being ignored, crying in the supermarket and people just walking the past, getting more and more confused, frightened, no one paying any attention, no one cares.
- ♥ Hmmm.... it feels very sad, doesn't it? What do you think the end result for that child would be? Do you think it's going to feel happy and positive at any point in life if this has happened time and again? Do you think it may start looking for places to feel safe and loved, perhaps getting the attention it needs through eating sugary comfort foods, alcohol, abusive substances?
- ♥ Relationships formed in adulthood can mirror rejections we felt as a child, so we take any love we can get to fill

the space… I hope I'm painting a picture of how this inner child might affect the outer world of an adult.

Whether or not you have any concept of the inner child or have maybe worked with the idea, don't worry; it may be new for you, but whatever your experience, it is fine to start from where you are and that is how we will work together in this chapter.

By using some simple thoughts you can sense the difference between engaging with, rather than ignoring, your inner child. There is no need to go into long psychological explanations, you can check all that out later if you want to. There really is no big secret of working with our inner child; all children are at their best with play, kindness and plenty of fun. I hope to share what has worked for me and how magical that journey has been. So, let go of patterns that have left you stuck somewhere feeling unworthy, helpless, depressed, or limited.

My Inner Child's Journey

I was lucky enough to find a connection with my inner child through being a children's yoga teacher. After working in television, film and running my own business, I was mentally and physically exhausted and decided on a career change at the age of thirty-one. I never intended to work with children or even be a yoga teacher but the universe gently guided me to what I believe is part of my life mission whilst I'm here on this planet.

I had suffered since my early teens but, living in the Staffordshire countryside in the 90s, depression and anxiety were not really talked about let alone treated. Had I known what I know now, my life would have been a very different experience; wanting to feel happier and free from anxiety was one driving force behind my career change.

I knew I had to change my lifestyle and what I did in the world; to make a difference and feel happy. One day I fell upon a magical practice called *Life Activation*, in the form of a one-to-one session with an energy healer from an ancient lineage. As I had long been very sensitive to energy, I was already interested in various teachings, had read about life activation and knew about magick schools. The work in the session was from an ancient mystery school, over 3000 years old in the lineage of King Salomon – and from here I began to feel better…

It was then that *Mini Me Yoga* was born. I decided that I would write a book to help children, a self-help book. After all, I had read loads of them as an adult and created a successful career from having done so; it has always confused me why we still teach children in a system that requires millions of adults to read self-help books?

My mission seemed clear, yet I had no words to spill onto paper. After much thought and many days, I realised that I needed to *do*, not write. Action was required, so I took the next step of my progression and healing by joining a two-day *Empower Thyself* class with the Salomon Lineage, which gave me the tools I needed to change direction. Slowly, it awakened parts I had forgotten existed and, after practising with my newly learned spiritual tools and meditation techniques, I decided to train as a kids' yoga teacher.

On this course, I began the emotional journey of acknowledging my inner child, although I had no idea how it would affect me. She was quite stubborn at the start; after all, I had ignored her for an awfully long time… but gradually she decided that she might like to play alongside the other trainees. At first, I felt awkward and shy as I tried to connect with her, as I had forgotten how to let go of my inhibitions. What surprised me is how quickly I forgave myself for hiding this part of me as an adult; and my inner child didn't hold onto the grudge either, fun was on the table and she chose to be in on it.

She began to feel happy and secure, loved and wanted, and from then on she was glad to be nurtured in my life, developing a really positive influence instead of trying to get my attention in unsupportive ways. This changed my life miraculously, so that I was confident to mix socially compared to the challenge I had felt attending social events just a few months before. To everyone else, I was still the happy, successful Kate. I know some of you reading this will know exactly what I'm talking about.

As our journey progressed something magical happened: my inner child started to teach me, she started to share her knowledge of how to have fun, showed me how to work with the children as a kids' yoga teacher, shared with me the things she quite liked. And guess what? The children in my class loved her and her ideas!

As time went by, I got better as a grown-up and started to work with parents and teachers, through a two-hour workshop on how they could bring a simple fifteen-minute yoga and mindfulness program to children. It was important to me to reach as many children as I could, which I could do more effectively by helping other grown-ups use these tools on a daily basis, rather than children only having access to them in my weekly yoga class.

When I shared these tools with the adults they eagerly wanted to share them with the children in their own life, believing they were doing it purely to help the children. Yes, of course, the fifteen minutes *Happy Healthy Kids Program* will help children... but here's the secret: the kids already get it! They already know how to play, have fun – they make no judgement. The magick that made the grown-ups feel so good inside was their own inner child being loved, acknowledged and allowed to have fun! Finally, I was really beginning to understand that JOY was the key to it all.

It occurred to me, very early on in *Mini Me Yoga*'s life, that the inner child of the grown-up who was playing with the child created a bonding experience that led to a quantum leap in healing. A quantum leap means the action of healing a many-layered situation, perhaps uprooting a thought that has been so deeply buried or inaccessible that it starts to cause negative patterns or habits in one's life.

Writing this chapter has given me the chance to tell the backstory of *Mini Me Yoga* and how it is used in twenty-four countries, reaching thousands of children per week. Its success is not just because kids love having fun, it is because our inner child, whatever age we are, is allowed to express itself and be acknowledged.

But does fun and being happy really make a difference?

We are lead to believe that being clever, a good student showing academic diligence is what really makes a difference in our lives. But that is not entirely true. We must have fun in our life – we are here to be happy, to feel joy! Of course, the hippies told us this many years ago, but this is not a New Age concept. It is at the heart of ancient teachings that have been shared with some of the most powerful leaders throughout time. But don't just take my word for it. I'm glad to report that there is a lot of science behind the concept of having fun and the effects of happiness on our lives. It has been well documented that happy people live longer, have longer marriages, are healthier and have more money!

When we feel happy we send signals to the cells in our body where chemicals are released that help us stay mentally and physically well. To achieve true homeostasis our bodies must be balanced in all aspects, and the correct hormone balance is a key aspect. Yes, that is right, having fun with kids or being child-like ourselves is one way to stay on top of the ageing game, live longer and have more cash in your pocket! Do you need any other excuses to start having more fun in your life?

I am so fascinated by this that I am currently studying for my PhD in Natural Integrative Medicine, which incorporates quantum physics' theories about how healing takes place through these fun experiences.

One interesting concept that quantum medicine explains is about wrong feeling. This doesn't mean we are incorrect in our feelings rather that we have created an idea from an experience that we perceived in a false way and which we now hold onto as a negative experience, pretty much like the word 'perfect' and how it shaped my life. The wrong feeling I created about perfection caused me a life of anxiety as a young child and teenager; because I could never reach perfect I was, in my own mind, never good enough on so many levels.

Quantum medicine shows us that we can, in fact, change wrong feelings through re-patterning our thoughts and emotions, and engaging our senses. Doing this we can create a quantum leap of healing when we engage with a practitioner, doctor or a child. If the practitioner, child or doctor believes in the process and is a glowing example of what you want to be – healthy, happy, loved etc. – you or the recipient can change that wrong feeling to aid healing at a deep level.

So, spending just fifteen minutes a day having fun with your inner child or any child in your life, helps us shift those negative thoughts or wrong feelings that are no longer serving us. The effects may be subtle at first, trust must be gained, but we will see results. When we have fun we start to see that depression lift, the negative voice in our head quieten down, sadness shifting, tiredness turns into feeling energetic… we see the magick happening in front of our eyes.

Your Turn. How Do I start?

You start by having the fun, of course! Sounds simple but write down five things that are fun and allow you to feel joy. When we get older we can lose sight of what we actually find fun, or indeed we have grown-up fun which involves drinking or late nights, which a small child or inner child doesn't flourish on. So you need to go back to the beginning and have fun like a child.

Children learn from us, so setting a good example of having fun each day will be a wonderful habit to show that even adults retain and acknowledge their inner child. It's really good for your mental, emotional and physical well-being and you may even decide that not being too serious and sophisticated all the time is a way to stay healthy, happy and focussed as we get older. Making sure that your inner child is never ignored means there will never be a basis for harmful, attention-demanding patterns to emerge.

I promised a few suggestions to help you on your way to connecting with that child inside your self. There are many exercises directed towards children in my *15 Minutes to Happy Healthy Kids Program*, which has seven steps offering different games to play and ways to adapt them, along with reasons to use them and how they will assist in your life. Sometimes we use Magick Yoga Cards which help with yoga poses and have myriad other uses which are revealed throughout the program. We all know that children love magic, fun and adventure, no different to your inner child. But here I share with you ideas about reaching out to your own inner child, that often forgotten and neglected but always needy and magical part of you that is waiting to be rediscovered and celebrated in your adult heart space.

It's Your Turn Now

Always the first step, you know what I'm going to say, is calming down from the world of outside demands and allowing yourself the freedom to be your remembered, innocent and unencumbered self – you may have fleeting memories of how you felt, on good days, as a child? When we are stressed from rushing or organising a million things at once, our inner child does not get the attention it needs. So ring-fence a few minutes each day to connect with your heart, using the simple but very powerful technique of bringing your awareness to those around you, not just family and friends but also perhaps those in an underprivileged community, or into the wider natural environment. Open your heart and connect with them with love, one at a time at first, forgiving old pain and letting go of stale thought patterns.

Coming Together

- ♥ Make yourself warm and comfortable, then place your hands on your heart, and take a moment to breathe quietly.
- ♥ See your heart full of love, excitement, joy. Make an ohmmm sound and feel your heart vibrate – this vibration allows you to direct your love out to anyone in the world, whether you know them or not and whatever the past history between you.
- ♥ Practice making the ohmmm sound, quietly at first – in your own way.
- ♥ Now, take a deep but relaxed breath and try directing your ohmmm vibrations outwards.
- ♥ First send out love to family members and those you love. The second ohmmm send out to the environment, your pet or favourite animal, rainbows or the rainforest –

it's your choice. The third ohmmm is sent to your local community or an area of the world in need of love.

- ♥ Note how you feel afterwards – maybe write it down.
- ♥ Keep practising – it works!

So, what does this exercise do? Well, you are utilising ground-breaking positive thinking techniques that empower our bodies with physical and emotional understanding. By consciously bringing a feeling like love into your heart, in its healing qualities and then sending it out into the world, it focuses attention on just how much you really believe the power in your heart can create new energy or change the old. Your revisited and trusting inner child is empowered to realise that it can make a difference and that its positive thoughts and actions can flow into the world. That child and you, its adult form, have been heard!

Notice how we send out love to our family. Not all families live in the same house, or even country, and this exercise is a wonderful tool for allowing us to connect, whenever we want and on a heart level, with children or significant people who are not physically present in our lives. We have a way of hooking into disagreements and obstacles then replaying them over and over until they escalate in our minds, because we haven't let go or forgiven. By sending out unconditional love, we can wash away those negative feelings and clean the path to forgiveness. I know that I never feel so bad after this practice, and usually find it in my heart to forgive, see a misunderstanding or realise I have taken words the wrong way.

You can extend the practice as far as you wish, connecting to animals from ants to elephants or plants from daisies to forests. As adults we can forget to enjoy the freedom and magnificence of nature, in the way we may have done when we were that child who is still part of us, so connecting our inner child with the natural world is rejuvenating and healing. It reminds us of our very first sense of environmental wonder. Send out love to people in your local community too, especially if you feel disconnected from them. You might see people every day but feel you don't know them well enough to speak, and you probably won't go up and hug a lonely stranger either, but you can send support and friendship this way, so raising a bond in your local community.

The physical aspect of the ohmmm is dynamic, affecting the thyroid and throat chakras. Through the vibration you produce from your own heart space you will clear those stuck emotions; things you wish you had said or done or those you regret. It has been well documented that ohming has an extreme calming effect on body and mind. Try it and you'll see. I know that after the three ohms that we practice with the kids in my classes, they feel calm, relaxed and ready for fun. It can happen for your child self too.

When Did You Last Dance?

Everyone's inner child loves to dance, so it is a soul freeing work out for all ages. The hurdle is often how to let go of that inner critical voice of self-consciousness and self-judgement. With children in my classes we use a pack of Magick Yoga Cards to create four music and dancing yoga games; you can purchase the cards and full e-learning on our website should you so wish.

But this time it's about you and the remembered child inside who may have been shy or fearful of letting go, or equally may have loved dancing, finding themselves accepted, unjudged, accepting others and deeply engaging with their creativity and physical self-expression through movement. You thought it was just dancing? As an adult it's about getting rid of the hang-ups and letting rip!

Choose music that is fun for your inner child – no one is going to comment or judge you on your choice – and something you can really move to. Dance can be great for bonding with your own children in which case they can help choose, but this time choose whatever suggests itself to how *you* want to feel. It doesn't matter if it's completely out of character for you; in fact, take a chance – nobody's looking! Dance till you feel as free as a toddler or a teenager, or your *self*. If you want to have a bit of fun, use our Magick Yoga Cards and stop the music every now and then to perform one of the poses, like this one for example:

The Dog Pose: just do it how it looks to you!

Mandala Art

Mindfulness and meditation are tools to help your inner child slow down and become aware of its own thoughts. They increase awareness and help us master our emotions, staying balanced and focussed in everyday life.

Meditation brings calm and peace. There are so many studies proving that meditation benefits all aspects of health, most notably changing our brain structure and allowing greater capacity to process and then retain information. You can use mandalas, guided stories and music as meditation tools if you are not used to the practice. Mandalas are symbolic of our wholeness and the circles of cosmic life inside and out. Here's one of my favourite mandalas for you to colour quietly, with focus and concentration; just let go of outside concerns and enjoy the silence.

Joy mandala

My Journey Since

Since I acknowledged my inner child, my path has enabled me to be kind to myself. I no longer drink alcohol, smoke, or engage with negative people or situations. I don't eat food with chemicals in... Yes, it's taken time to reach this point. But my inner child is happier if she doesn't wake up with a hangover or feel irritable from sugar in her food. I have grown to know myself better and discover what works for me through having connected with my inner child. Each day, as my inner child grows, I check in to understand what now make her happy. All children change, adapt and grow – so does your inner child!

The best thing of all is that I get to share this growth with kids. When I connect to them through my inner child I can sense that they feel safe to be who they really are: not sensible, clever, well-behaved. They can let down their guard and be THEM!

This is the most magical gift I can offer a child and one I hope they will share with others as they grow up. Children do not judge, see colour or race, so I believe we can change the world and live in peace if we encourage children to stay with that lack of judgement – connecting with who they really are.

Stepping Out

One of my greatest gifts is being step parent to a wonderful boy, sharing these tools with him during his early years and learning how well these practices work for parent, child and inner child. Healing my inner child was key to my journey as a step parent. I wasn't prepared for parenting when I met my husband, but my stepson had just turned three, my husband was very much part of his life and one of the things that I fell in love with was his dedication to his son and how full of love and happiness his child was to meet me.

As a step parent I found out how hard it can be to fit into the role that is needed but, by healing my inner child, I was able to have fun and not pass on my own childhood issues to my stepson. But the connection we created from the beginning of our journey together has built a strong foundation and as we move into his young adult years, that foundation of love remains strong. Do we still do yoga together now he is thirteen? Not so much, but he was there right from the beginning so I talk to him about *Mini Me Yoga* and how it's developed. On holidays we do beach yoga together, he knows how to breathe and stay calm when he gets stressed, he knows how to manage his own energy, his inner child is listened to – a gift that will shape the rest of his adult life and my life too.

I look forward to hearing about your experiences and perhaps even seeing videos of you having fun.

Enjoy your journey!

Inner child mandala

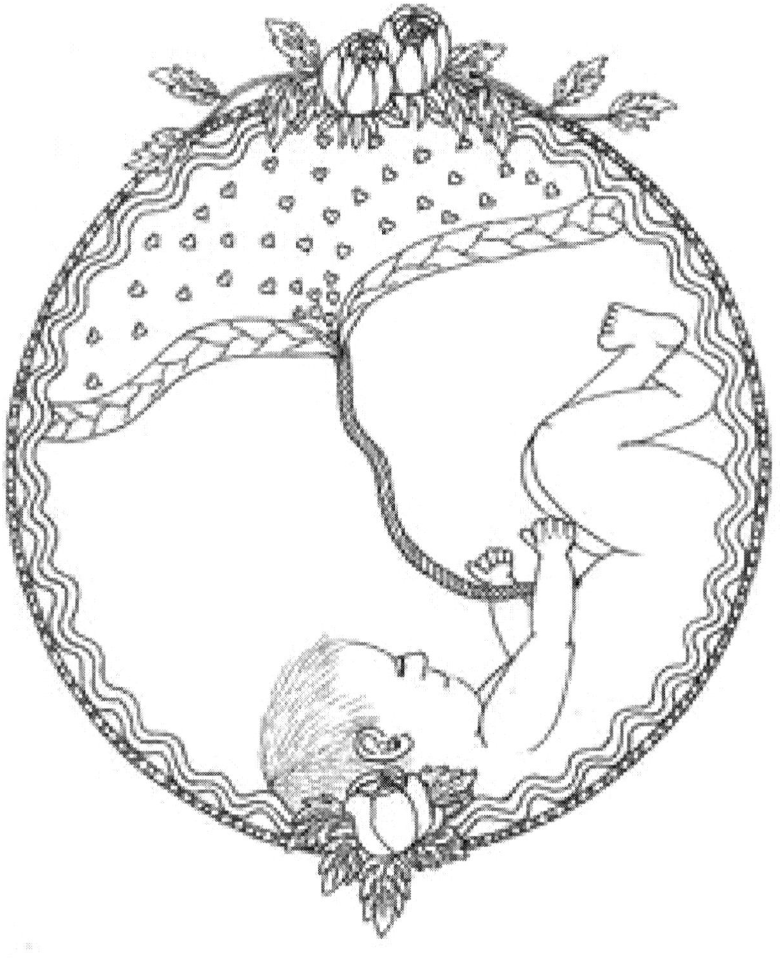

Deeper Faith

Laura

OVER THE PAST YEARS I HAVE WILLINGLY SURRENDERED and accepted that, in order for me to really live the life that I desire, it is vital for me to up-level my faith factor to a higher degree and this means believing in myself, that life wants me to succeed and that what I am doing is loved and accepted. Yes, embracing a feeling of faith, regardless of whatever is going on around me, is my biggest mission. Training myself to live in faith through the toughest times strengthens my heart, so that I know life is always on my side. I believe that we are each here to live out, express and fulfil our highest calling, whatever that may mean for us individually. There is no right or wrong way. There is constant change and I also believe that spiritual law and order are in constant action. With this deepening faith, each step I take brings me closer towards my world of desires and dreams. Faith is the glue.

I can't give you a secret to how to acquire this sense of faith that I am so grateful for; it just took me a lot of soul searching and an even bigger willingness and desire to detect and change my old unhelpful thoughts, mindset and feelings. I can, though, offer a great exercise to help guide you towards feeling faith and releasing fear.

When you are feeling out of control, just remind yourself that it is always happening for a reason and for your highest good. Whatever is happening, be prepared to thank life, as the universe only ever gives us what it knows we can handle and we are BIGGER than any situation that arises. When you have some time, silence and space...

Fear to Faith

- ♥ Get plenty of paper, a pencil and be in silence.
- ♥ First ask yourself, are you willing RIGHT NOW to place deep faith into your heart and mind... yes or no? Either answer is

okay, this simply gives you a measure of your faith so you can work from this point.

- Close your eyes and bring your awareness to your situation.
- Ask yourself: *How am I feeling? Are there fear thoughts running in my mind? Am I ready to forgive?*
- Now, write down your thoughts, as many as you can. Have a look at what you've written. Can you see that this is only your perception of the situation? If someone else came along with double the problems they may look at you right now and show you how well you are doing.
- Now I invite you to collect your statements together into similar groups e.g. fear, feeling unsafe, not having enough, being unloved and so on.
- In pencil write out a statement for each group, one that encompasses all your feelings and thoughts about the state of how you believe things are.
- Let's call these your *fear statements*
- Now, on clean paper, I invite you to write out another statement spelling out the exact opposite of your fear statements. For example, *I am fearful of not having enough money → There is more than enough and I have complete faith in life.*

- ♥ This is your new Faith Mantra. Begin it with I Am..., I Have..., I Now..., keep it in the present tense and read it over and over, many times a day as you visualise it happening.
- ♥ Now check over your old story, the fear statement, the one you think you're experiencing. Take a moment to thank it for the picture it gives because you can now let go of it – then rip it up into tiny tiny pieces, bin it or burn it (safely).
- ♥ You could also do this on toilet paper and flush it!

So, your new deep faith message is just that, a message. Alone it can support you to create a new belief system – practiced together with visualisation and prayer it will turbo you into your new self. Repeat this statement with deep faith and feeling, in the knowing that it's already done and that you are the most powerful creator of your life. Visualise yourself as you desire to be and know that, by doing this, you are activating your conscious mind to connect with its subconcious and bring the new story to reality.

It takes more than faith because, in essence, you are tricking your subconscious and it is so important to turn your focus and attention away from what you are living right now. You are re-programming your life with new thoughts and it takes a heap of patience, self-will and determination to bypass your present experiences in order to create a new reality within.

You can change things from within (however bad they might seem) by looking at all the good around you NOW, and you can set up a foundation of new feelings, thoughts and beliefs. You are the power of your world and, from inside, you can transform anything. Nelson Mandela released himself to freedom with deep forgiveness and using this practice. The power of spirit within you is the ultimate force that fashions this life; why would it stop at you?

Knowing deep within your heart that you *are enough* can be seen as your first gleaming stepping stone over wild rapids that could otherwise pull you away from reaching the shore safely. It takes practice, patience and a whole heap of self-belief to change your self-talk. Let's face it, if you believe in yourself at this stage, in all ways, you open the door to believe in everything that stems from within you. Even when you have a passion, a dream, a vision it is still easy to get stuck in a false picture of *now* and lose faith. It is vital to keep faithfully laying the track, building on that foundation of staying in your truth, for the next step to be simple and easy.

Knowing you are enough in your *mind* is very different to really knowing and feeling it in your *heart and soul*, where the work becomes embedded. My desire for you is to fully experience the feeling of being enough. Simply stop where you are right now, put aside the 'to do' list for a few moments, close your eyes and visualise a rich golden light pouring over you, it loves and accepts you and knows you are here, right now, in your greatness and magnificence. Picture yourself bathed in this light and allow yourself to *feel amazing*, being comforted and held safely in its love. This light is the highest part of you, always present, and it is my truest desire for you to be living in it. Whatever is going on in your world, you can always come back to the knowing, unconditional acceptance of this light. Oh, one more thing, this light is infinite. There is so much light that it couldn't fit into our known universe – it will never run out. It is here always, abundantly, and for every one of us in all ways.

This is the light of *You Are More Than Enough*. It's up to you to use this light to fully and bask in its glory – let it flow as the vibrant energy of your magnificence!

Sing your own song with love and faith and know that as you reach out, life holds your hand and guides you with all its might to live your dreams fully for your highest good. And so it is.

Processing Peace

There are so many devoted causes and charities working for peace and here for the greater good of the planet, and I so admire their work and intentions. However, my work is more concerned with each of us as individuals living in and creating our personal lives through the energy of peace. Peace is a natural spiritual energy, an eternal energy and state of being, and it's here to stay! As humans we have the power to be vessels of peace in our own lives and to choose the energy of peace in our thoughts and actions. What does living in peace mean for you? Does it mean having harmony at home with your family and children; does it mean calmness in your day and faces smiling back at you from everyone you see and meet; does it mean living in safety? It's important to work out what peace really means to us as individuals and to begin the process of *being* in a peaceful state as first port of call. All that we are is mirrored back at us in every way, so actually *being* the peace process that we desire to experience for the world is the most vital first step. Who doesn't crave world peace? For all that do, there is always an opportunity to begin the process from right where we are, here and now, to develop clarity about how we can be more peaceful, calm, loving and harmonious, firstly with ourselves, so that the calm energy will automatically ripple out. Launch the peace process with YOU, no one else, just you. Map out in your mind what it means to live in inner peace. It could mean changing the way you talk to yourself, creating harmony in your living space, turning off the TV, or turning on the TV! Love yourself and allow this to be your way. You know it's impossible to be anything for others until we can firstly be that quality for ourselves. I believe this is just how life works. Yes, it's vital to want peace for our planet, but peace is just a vibration and, like any form of energy, it must be used correctly to be appreciated. We are keyholders for peace, so by consciously intending to live in peace we align with that energy. Screaming at the dog and then signing a petion for world peace is living in a divided house, not a harmonious state – not helpful.

Now, in honesty, I can say that once we have children in our lives there are so many opportunities that arise, as a loving mama, for differences of opinion! Especially as our bundles of joy enter their teenage years and build their own creative set of rules. You might well ask how you can walk around the house OOOOHMMMMMMing in peace with an incense stick in the burner, ignoring the over-the-top messy bedroom, the trail of teen social arrangements and constant disagreements over time curfews, yet still live in total peace within. The thing is, we know it's not easy to work through the negotiations of a determined 'tween or teen and still live in our truth, so I see setting boundaries as an important part of creating our own peace process. There's no reason to scream and shout when unforseen situations arise, we can as easily respond to situations calmly rather then react in anger and it's all about being aware of our intentions to find and travel in that place of harmony within.

Just as essential as creating an inner world of peace in mind, is knowing that we are not here to fix everything we feel needs to be fixed nor to become peacemaker for others' actions or behaviours. Forgiveness is the key to letting go and enables peace to flourish but it is not our responsibility to mend other people's broken lives nor to make things perfect for all; that's simply people pleasing. Living *in* peace is a conscious choice to radiate and vibrate peace as a harmonious loving state, which takes practice, patience and willingness to step back, not always so easy with a 'tween pushing the boundaries, but absolutely necessary for wellbeing in our own world.

Creative Living – Use the Power of Your Imagination

Think about it, everything in this life exists because of an idea… everything you see around you is here because someone, somewhere had the idea to create it. Nature exists because it's a ready-made idea. It certainly wasn't mankind's idea, it was an idea that came from the unseen force of life. You're reading this book right now that I had the idea to create and bring to form. It took me nine months, a lot of love and devotion and six other women to join with my idea along the way. What shall I have for dinner tonight? Now there's a thought, the beauty of this one is that you can choose, well it might be that you are restricted because of money to pay for a three course gourmet meal right now or you may not be able to find your favorite pasta in the village you live in, but you can choose in your mind to create the meal in some form and focus on bringing it to your table, it's an idea that takes shape because of your focus.

Living creatively is far from living as an out there artist, musician or inspired writer, this is living *through* creativity, for me living creatively means to use the power of my imagination to enable me to design my desires, to use my mind to paint the picture I want for my life and to plant seeds of faith, knowing that it all exists for me as I am ready to accept and receive it. Living creatively is allowing myself the pleasure of bringing to life my dreams, feeling fulfilled and excited that my ideas can run free and have space to flourish with real permission to colour my world, all from my secret place within where no one else has access unless I care to let them in. What I realise more and more is the absolute importance of allowing myself the unleashed pleasure of embracing my imagination and allowing my ideas to become guiding lights that inspire me to create, to play, to experiment with what I feel I want for my life. I believe that ideas are under-rated and that we are only used to expressing ideas that seem acceptable. In my world all schools would have IDEAS GCSE's and A Levels. I think that our children could very much benefit from ideas lessons and that they have such a natural tendancy to create that this could allow for untold discoveries and inventions in later years. My daughter, having learning differences, has the most random ideas for life and I feel blessed that she can come up with such creative ways of thinking, not just out of the box – there is no box.

As a mama on a mission you are called to embody your ideas and allow them, however nonsensical they may feel, to enter your world. Bring out your ideas with shameless pride and move them from your mind into your life.

What so often happens is that we have an idea but the old comfy part of us, that doesn't believe in our capabilities, pipes up and subconsciously tells us that it's impossible and asks who we think we are to even think such a thing or imagine we deserve to? More often than not, we listen to this voice and actually believe its controlling limitations but my big message to you now is to IGNORE THE VOICE and accept the idea as divine inspiration, however small, large, insignificant, outrageous or unrealistic it may seem to you. Infuse your idea with love, honour it with a *yes* and sit down with it for a while, allowing it into your inner world; you've had the notion, so you own it and it could be the idea that singularly shifts your whole world, so give it the chance that it deserves. Your ideas may be worthy of great placement in your life to create and live the life of your dreams or they may be just a stepping stone for something greater, so here's my Five Step Suss-out for inspired ideas.

Firstly, buy a gorgeous notebook, small enough to fit in your bag and beautiful enough to feel great about pulling out. It's not about the price tag, it's about the way it makes you feel.

Your Five Steps to Seeding Ideas

1. Each time you have an idea, write it in your book with the date. Keep track of them as the same idea may pop up regularly over time.

2. Contemplate that idea and visualise the idea happening in your mind as if it's already happened – allow yourself to feel the feelings that arise.

3. Any feeling other than excitement and anticipation is a good indicator that your heart isn't really in it, so put the idea to one side – for now.

4. If the idea excites you then live with it for a while and really allow yourself to embrace it in your heart and begin to feel that it's a part of your life. It may be a creative project that you are ready to birth, a country that you'd like to visit, a place you are called to be in. Know that if it is calling you then it will demand your attention and belief.

5. If an idea feels right, start by writing down steps you can begin taking to move closer to it and bring it into your life, for example, if you are drawn to writing a book but feel unsure and unconfident, just buy a writing book, a pen and begin to write. If you are thinking of visiting another country, begin researching that place and plan the trip in your mind.

Above all, cherish your ideas as creative inner messages that will move you towards living your most fulfilled and creatively expressed life, which really is why we are here – to love it, to live it and to go for it!

Hearts mandala

The HeART of Writing

Zoë Owl

WRITING IS AN ART FORM much like artistic painting; there are layers, depth, shades and tones of words, phrases, sentences, paragraphs and pages of creation, each with different strokes of the pen or brush. Some are light, others more deep, depending on what the artist is creating. Not all writing is soft pastel pinks and baby blue hues, sometimes writing can convey dark crimson and deep violet palettes. Much like music, writing has rhythm; a beat and a pulse all of its own. Writing can be baked in a multitude of flavours that tantalise the taste buds, stimulate the ear drums and focus the pupils of the eyes. Words are not merely *just* words on a page, it is how they are constructed and put together that makes the whole greater than the sum of its (word) parts, much like a painted picture or piece of music. Creators are experimental in freely trying out different things, modalities and approaches, in how they choose to express themselves. At the very heART of creative writing and journalling is free expression and the ability to fully embrace the truth of who we are. This requires not denying any less favourable aspects of ourselves because they do not conform to another's ideas of how we should live our life, and/or society's ideals and judgement of what is 'normal', and 'not normal'. Writing from the heART is free-flow streams of truth that come from your own personal experiences. Creative expression needs freedom, much as the bird needs the air in order to fly.

This chapter focuses on the heART of journalling in particular because it is such a personally powerful, therapeutic, and life transforming creative tool, that you can use to change your life. Many people cast the process of personal journalling aside because they fail to understand just how essential it is to creating the life of your dreams and desires. Neuro-psychologists have measured that the human brain has between 50,000-70,000, with an average of 60,000, thoughts per day. This figure breaks down as a quantifiable 35-48 thoughts per minute! With such a vast quantity of mind matter to process, we need space and tools to do this effectively. Many of those 60,000 thoughts per day will of course be repeating thoughts that are stuck on a continuous loop, linked in to our limiting self-beliefs and programming patterns. In re-running the scripts in our minds, that is *our story* that we tell ourselves and others over and over again, we clock up a mass of mind-based material to store and sort out in our heads. Other thought bundles that we have may be more scattered and fragmented. Therefore, it is entirely logical that the thought creator may feel an emotional need to have some integration, structure and order around these sometimes wild, disturbing or unwanted thoughts.

What Is Journalling?

At the heART of journal keeping is making a safe home for our private, and sometimes very deep personal thoughts, that we are not always given the opportunity to openly share and bounce off with others. Thoughts are very powerful because they are energies that drive us and our resulting cognitive-behavioural and emotional patterns. Our thoughts are constantly transforming, updating and travelling with us, journeying through our lives. As we navigate our life pathways and have more varied experiences, so we also need to check in with our neural thoughts and current ideas and update these accordingly where necessary, depending upon our new discoveries and challenges. Thoughts are energy and energy is constantly changing and moving, so journalling helps us to get a grip on this fast flow, to process and to reflect on our deepest and most private thoughts, that may not always be fully conscious to our everyday levels of awareness. Our levels of awareness are also constantly fluctuating on a daily basis, so journalling as a direct response to this shifting process, offers a concrete tool and space to view our fleeting and repeating thoughts. It helps us to notice patterns, identify changes that we have made, or are in need of making and to view our overall progress. Journalling offers the opportunity to orientate and integrate ourselves in a very intimate way. For example, you may write things in your personal journal that you have never told your best friend, mother or lover, or even self-confessed. The heART of journalling helps us to understand our own lives that are determined by our thoughts, allowing for reflection and a space to view how we are leading and orchestrating our lives as our own director or conductor.

Emotional intelligence at a basic core level is about knowing how we feel, and self-managing what to do with our feelings. As fundamental as this type of emotional intelligence is towards leading a healthy balanced life, it is not yet current practice to teach our population how to identify, process and handle feelings, as much as the emphasis is on to strive for high IQ intelligence scores for example, in mainstream curriculum. Yet all of us, have at times experienced inner turmoil and confusion at not knowing how we feel towards a certain individual or about a particular life encounter, that can throw our inner radar askew. Whether this is because we have not been effectively taught good emotional intelligence practices, or because adapting to change in general is so central to the human experience of growth, journalling can help. If you cannot understand what you are feeling, if your feelings are blocked or are jumbled and mixed up, privately writing them down can assist you to get a better grasp of them. If you hear so many different voices in your head, for instance your mother's or father's words ringing in your ears, as well as your own voice, and you are not sure which voice to listen to, journalling can help you distinguish which path to take.

Effectively, journalling is a way of getting to know yourself and to know what is yours, and what belongs to others. Katie Dalebout, a self-confessed *wellness and journalling nerd* and author of a new journalling self-help book was interviewed recently on a Radio Hay House Telesummit. Katie described her eating-disordered background and said that journalling can '*act as a plunger, helping to remove all the junk that is not needed, all of the grime on top of the stagnant pond, in order to get to the clear water and more creative clarity underneath*'. Journalling offers a process of learning what is beneficial to keep and what is destructive and limiting and therefore goes into the discard pile, so as to maintain healthy mental and emotional functioning.

Living in the modern world with the most advanced technologies offering vast amounts of information at our fingertips, means we are bombarded with material from the outside world trying to get inside our heads. Whether we seek out this information or not, advertisers make sure that our exposure levels as consumers are kept at a constant high. There is a mass of material therefore to filter and sift to make sense of what is necessary, valuable and beneficial to us as individuals, for our loved ones and communities. Journal keeping offers a way to consolidate all that we are thrown by others and that which we pick up on, as well as seek out for ourselves. In this modern age we are overloaded with stimuli that we need to make sense of and try to take some form of control over. Journalling therefore offers an outlet to take some physical notes, rather than just relying on mental notes which of course are subject to memory loss, bias and influence. Psychologists have demonstrated that thoughts in the brain which travel down through the arm, hand and to the writing fingers, encode memory into deeper forms of consciousness, compared to not writing thoughts down onto paper. Hence the saying that 'geniuses write things down!'. This is particularly beneficial to women in modern society of course, who are typically great multi-taskers in juggling varied roles of managing family, professional business and busy social lives. The journal keeper offers themselves a space in which to integrate and consolidate all the information and feelings towards a certain aspect. This can impact upon the many different areas of our lives. Crucially the journalling will also help to highlight where it is that we are in and out of balance in our busy lives, that we may not have otherwise noticed.

Hopes and Dreams

There is a variety of different types of journalling that can be used for very different reasons, serving different purposes. For example, classically, there is a Hopes and Dreams type of journalling that is futuristic planning of desires and aspirations. This type of journalling is intention-setting and can be used to capture and write down structured and concrete goal setting. There is also a more free-flowing type of healing journalling that offers a place to purge and outpour the deeper, darker thoughts and musings that we may have that perhaps just need to be let out, or emotions that we want to release. This kind of journalling tends to be more fast and furious in style, and perhaps the creator may even tear it up or burn it after writing to fully release. There may be no intention to hold on to or keep this journal output. It is often done without thinking too much about the content and detail too closely, but rather having an emphasis on being raw and real about it and just purging it up and out. This is a very therapeutic style of writing.

Compliments Journal

Another type of therapeutic writing is a compliments journal that serves to nurture your perception and memories of the good moments in your life by taking some notes when you are feeling positive and upbeat to later re-read when you're perhaps not feeling so positive. It is good perspective training. This type of journalling serves almost like an emotional investment pick-me-up for a rainy grey-mood day. To cite a personal example, I sporadically write down very positive and deeply moving compliments both from people that I know and do not know, ones they have gifted to me in magical treasured moments.

Then if I happen to be struggling with self-worth or self-esteem issues on other days, sometimes years later, I can re-read my compliments journal to remind myself of how others have perceived me and actively commented. This is a very powerful pick-me-up for me because I know they are authentic and were genuinely given. It also reminds me of those happy memories at the time the compliments were given. So it's a double winner method.

This is similar to the *happiness jar* journalling method, of writing down on post-it notes all the happy events and memories that happen to you throughout the year, which may include positive compliments people have given you, and collecting them in a jar or treasure box. Then at the following New Year you can read all of the year's highlights to set you up for an even more positive year ahead.

Gratitude Journal

Keeping a gratitude journal is a very positive stand-alone type of journalling, with emphasis on being grateful for all the events and aspects of our lives, helping us to see the joy, beauty and help that exists all around us, even when we are struggling to see existence or evidence of positivity. A creative journal may be a more work-focussed type of journalling, such as professional blogging and social media posting that follows and weaves with the creator's thought patterns and themes of interest. Dream journals are popular too, often kept by the bedside to capture the unconscious messages brought to our conscious attention via our dream states. Emotional journalling may stem from dealing with a strange situation, event or person that presents the need to explore more around how we feel about it or are reacting towards it. Akin to when we feel the need to speak with a friend, when we are grasping what is happening to us and how we are affected. There is also a Note Form Prompting type of journalling, that may involve writing down one word, a few words or sentences of ideas or emotions, or perhaps something we take note of that we need to further explore later. Technology is useful for this kind of journalling, for instance by using the *Notes* application on smart phones. However, the old-fashioned pen and paper notebook can still be useful for jotting down notes. As you can see, journalling is not one thing, there are many different ways in which to journal.

Personally speaking, I have employed a wide variety of journalling techniques, some are very clinical in note-taking style and on a particular theme of interest, such as the number of British inmates at the peak of the prison crisis and my professional observations and opinions on this. Other journalling ran to my deepest, darkest private thoughts on my reasons for existence and being here on the earth. That's not all in one day of course, but over a lifetime period of approximately thirty years of regular journalling. My writing ramblings all started with tormented teenage diaries and first early love letters to the school love rat and it all went from there really. Along the journey I have also conscientiously taken note of every book that I want to read, play and film that I want to see, musical band that I want to hear and place of interest that I want to visit and travel to. I have learned in my years of flowering wisdom to keep all these types of jotting in one place of reference. It just makes for a simpler and easier life.

Why Journal?

Some of the benefits of journalling have already been touched upon in exploring what journalling actually is in the previous section. To recap, journalling provides a central, intimate home to reflect and process our many, repeated, deepest and most private thoughts and emotions. The writing outlet allows us to get in touch with our feelings and thoughts, and to be more conscious of them and their patterning. We begin to get to know ourselves better when we journal because it affords us the opportunity to be more organised in sorting through which cognitions and emotions we want to keep, being true to our own inner voice, and those that we wish to discard from our busy working brains. This decluttering process then helps us to focus more coherently, and to live more balanced and healthier lives.

Furthermore, it offers a great aid to our decision-making processes. It helps us tune into our intuition, our deeper, inner feminine wisdom, and is also an optimal method for helping us to be in the present moment. When you are journalling, you are very much there in that moment, writing about the topic you are thinking about; you are present. Journalling also helps us to explore and find our *own* inner voice. If we find, for example, that we are seeking answers externally, by constantly asking others for their opinions or even approval, then we are not listening to our *own* inner truth and voice. Journalling gives you an opportunity to reflect upon what your own thoughts and ideas are towards any given subject. If you suffer from any confusion in your decision-making, a good technique to use is to write a pro and con list, of how you imagine that you would feel if either option A or option B came about. Journalling used in this way gives you the experience to write about how you *want* to feel; this impacts directly on every decision you make. Being aware of where we are situated in our own journey of life, enables us to more readily understand and navigate where it is that we *want* to go, or move towards. In other words, journalling helps us take stock and switch directions more fluidly, to become better masters of our own world. If we organize our thoughts better, rather than just allowing ourselves to go around in looped repeating patterning, with self-limiting thoughts circling in our heads, then we can more readily become the masters of our own destiny.

There are enormous therapeutic benefits to journalling, it is effectively free therapy. There is no one better to really open up to and let yourself and your thoughts free streamline with, than a blank, non-judgmental page! With full respect to the wide variety of professionals with their services on offer (myself included) that all have their place and many benefits to offer clients, each person already has all of the answers within themselves, and is their own best self-expert. The navigating task (which may sometimes require the assistance of a particular trained professional) is to work through what is blocking a person from accessing and hearing their own answers, wisdoms and lessons. It is very therapeutic to purge thoughts and raw emotions onto the page as a form of emotional release. Rather than holding on to the emotion, that can keep you trapped, possibly in victim mode. By writing down or typing out your thoughts and emotions, you make them more real, because they are then right there in front of you, in bold black and white, to explore, see and acknowledge. Often we might instinctively choose to do this in the form of diary writing for example, but this approach is also more formally taught in intuitive types of training, that wisely encourage us to detach and thus feel more free from intense emotions that can keep us locked into the drama of them. For instance, teachings from the

Buddhist perspective encourage soul seekers to live through their consciousness rather than through their emotions. It is very empowering to write in free flow streams, without any fear of judgement or comeback. When we use journalling in this way as a form of deep self-reflection, it is a very powerful tool to help us take stock of our lives and look back on how we have grown and developed over the years. It shows how the rich tapestry of our lives has unfolded and the patterns in which our interests have woven together, in ways that are difficult to have earlier predicted or possibly even have imagined. If we can agree that the universe, or the powers that be, has a grand master plan with everything all figured out, that we are a part of, then journalling helps to document and see the various different stages of that plan unfolding. Journalling assists in breaking down the complex into the simple to make it more manageable.

How Best To Journal?

The heART of journalling is not about being or conforming to a certain way, it is however, about giving free space to your thoughts and feelings in a way that feels safe to do and makes sense to you. There is no perfect way to do it. You have all the answers within you, so journalling is simply a tool to use to retrieve the information already contained within, in order to obtain the answers sought. How you use that tool is entirely personal and individual to you. It is basically a way to give space to your thoughts, emotions and feelings, to help make better sense of them, and to track your personal growth changes. Life is all about change and we are constantly transforming, so journalling provides an opportunity to check in with yourself, to help you take a step back and reflect on where you have been and where you are going. Journal keeping may serve as a way to be more conscious of your goals being reached and then resetting new aims and intentions accordingly. On the other hand, journalling may also be used therapeutically, in working towards accepting parts of yourself or your daily reality that is uncomfortable or uncertain, that you seek to change.

The best kind of journalling will be honest and open; revealing the soul bare, with raw emotions and feelings, that are sometimes dark, ugly, confused and hurting. The most effective healing will always include embracing all aspects of the human psyche, the darker shadow shades of the rainbow spectrum, as well as the lighter ones. Journal keeping allows these darker hues a space to get out from the confinement of the human brain and the stigma of not being regarded as socially acceptable matter. Once down on the page, words can be observed, explored and seen for what they are in the light of day. The journal is the most non-judgmental therapist or friend you could ever have and not to be secretive with. If you are not ready to confess a thought or emotion to your therapist or confidant for example, you can always write it down on paper, to *talk* out the feelings and emotions attached.

Speaking from personal experience, I have found this type of *get-it-off-your-chest journalling* to be very effective, especially when writing about traumatic events or major life changes. I have also witnessed many women attending a women's support circle benefit from this practice. A few years ago, I used to work as a mentor for Hestia the charity that supports women and children through an aptly named weekly support group called The Butterfly Project. As part of our events program we had a very established women's coach, Felicity Okolo, visit us to run an eight week course of *It Is My Life and I Am In Charge* recovery programme, adapted from her same titled book, with our attending women participating including myself as a volunteer. The women's coach asked us to literally write out our story, that is the story that we tell ourselves, our memories of what happened to us, with all the details and emotions that we felt at the time. This exercise served as an emotional purging to get that old story out of our systems that had remained stuck for so long, so we could begin to work on rewriting a new story for ourselves. The story of our lives that we wanted to experience and to see come about, with us as the writers and directors of our own lives. It was very empowering to personally experience and also to observe the direct changes that the women made to their own lives and to see them bloom in their personal transformation. This particular tool offers the writer the opportunity to self-coach and self-soothe. It is much like *dump* writing, where no one has to ever read it, but getting it all up off the chest, out of the body and down on the page to be explored and healed is the main purpose. The dumped produce can then be burned or torn up afterwards for the ultimate beneficial release effect. This is also similar to the method of writing a *pretend letter* to a person you are in conflict with, that you can safely write from a distance, and have your say on the page, without ever having to necessarily deliver the letter to that person. This can be extremely helpful with clearing stale or stuck emotions and blockages, serving much like a cathartic cleansing.

In the beginnings of my grey-hair wiser days, I started to write poetry, deep soul healing poetry that came directly from the cavities and shadows of my being, it certainly wasn't fluffy bunnies and unicorns! It was dark despair and slaughtered, raw core-wounding pain that spilled out onto the pages like a drained upside down carcass hanging, exposed and lifeless on a hook in the abattoir. I spilled my guts onto the page and purged. And purged. I also painted at this time, with deep purple messy paints that allowed my emotional wounding and bruising to come out and be expressed. I kept going with this until the lighter shades of the prism spectrum started to come through, and then with healing time, came the fluffy bunnies and unicorns. What I had skilfully developed was balance, not just in my writing that I had used as a free therapy tool, but in my life per se. To be balanced in natural equilibrium is to be healthy, happy and wise. Just like Mother Nature knows with her seasons and cycles of life. The thing to remember if you're in a winter or an early autumn/fall rhythm is that it will pass. Nothing lasts forever, not even diamonds (sorry Dame Shirley Bassey). So if you're having one of your darker days, or even longer periods, just stick with it, be with it as it is coming up for healing; whatever it is, it is seeking your attention and focus. This is the ultimate time to go within and to write! I went on to self-publish some of my poems in my first book titled *SOULutions: Soul Healing Poetry To Set Yourself Free* as I wanted to share my healing journey for it to be of benefit and value to others walking their own path.

To freely write away at your heart's content and have your free spill is liberating. To get it out and down on the page detaches its energy from you, somewhat. So, it's there in black and white staring back at you, stark and obvious, with no room for denial manoeuvre because it is what it is and that's that. This is the therapeutic heART of writing. Raw and real. No soft baby pinks and baby blue hue fluffy edges, this is crimson blood red. This is natural woman. This is wild and untamed feminine in all her glory. Magnificently exploring herself in the privacy of her own streaming thoughts and capturing them from heart and mind and pulling them down onto paper to be seen, heard, felt, explored, mutilated and healed. The trick of the heART is to not be frightened by what comes up, but rather to just allow. Surrender yourself to the flow of emotions and thoughts that stir and fester below society's socially acceptable benchmark of how it is reinforced that a woman should be expected to behave, do, think, feel or say. Take off all of those social girdles when you are free-writing from your heart because your heart and soul know the truth, the truth of your experience of how she wants to communicate with you. Only you, yourself alone, can hear your own inner voice from your higher and wiser self that is for your benefit to hear her. What does she say? What does she feel? Write it down!

Sometimes a more masculine style of journalling may be more appropriate, that is less like the feminine form of exploring in taking the long way around. Perhaps a more direct, rational and practical method, such as spider-graphing or item bullet-point listing, for example, may be more relevant. This is the Venus-Mars effect in the different styles of writing. Mental processing and cognition tends to be more in the masculine realm, whereas feelings and emotions attached to those corresponding thoughts are sentiments more in the feminine realm. Both are necessary and effective, and are most complementary when working well together in balance. We all think and we all feel, but just in different balanced ways and at different times in various contexts. Journal keeping helps you to be mindful of your patterning. If you tend to write in a certain way more often, this in itself can be very revealing to you as journal keeper, as to how balanced your writing styles are. The style of how you write is naturally mirror reflective of what is going on in your inner world. It is healthy to take stock and check in with yourself in working towards a positive balance of adopting and being in touch with both styles in an emotionally intelligent way.

What if you find yourself staring at a blank page with writer's block?

The best thing to do in this potential situation is to ask yourself a different prompt question, that is phrased in a more positive way to entice and elicit a more positive experience. Try a different angle, a different approach and style of journalling. For example, if you are feeling overwhelmed at not knowing where to start, or feeling fearful of the amount of *free spill* content, perhaps try writing a single word emotion that you feel daily, one in the morning when you wake to start your day, and a one-word emotion that you feel in the evening, following your day's experiences. With time, you can then map and track these emotions, looking for any patterning they reveal. You may find yourself expanding on these singular word emotions into multiples, or phrases and longer sentences. If I can draw on my own experience of this, several years ago I began a daily gratitude diary of things that happened in my everyday experience that I was grateful for. At first I began listing ten things every day as part of my routine practice. My gratitude listing increased gradually, by a few items consistently, and the more aware I was becoming of just how grateful I was, even with the very simple and most basic things in my life, the more gratitude poured out of me and the more items I was able to write down. Gratitude is an emotion. To be thankful is very humbling and the more I tuned into this emotion, the more aware I became of it being present in my world and the more and more grateful I naturally became. A self-fulfilling prophecy if you can think of it this way. It worked and so much so, that I now routinely write thirty-three daily gratitudes and no two days are ever the same! Writing is essentially natural to all of us in the first world countries of the twenty first century (where illiteracy is thankfully very rare), we can all write, and every one of us has an interesting and personal story to tell. The skill is to creatively experiment and not fixate on a certain way being right, and another being wrong. It is whatever works for you, you are Younique!

The most challenging journey that we ever take is the royal road within the self, and from the head to the heart. Journalling assists us to get our thoughts healthy and aligned with our emotions, with conscious awareness. This is when we begin to *heal-thy self* and become a healthy balanced whole. It is most helpful if we can think outside the box and not have any preconceived ideas of what form or shape our writing expression will birth in. Be open. Surrender to and allow what comes to the surface. Let your ideas, thoughts and emotions flow freely and let them surprise you in ways that are real, connected at core to you and so are authentic in whatever shape, colour or depth they come in. Allow them to be expressed freely and then sit back and watch for the magic of what unfolds.

And so it is that I am going to ask you to put aside preconceived ideas or experiences of how you think poetry 'should be', 'is' or 'is not' that perhaps you were unwisely and dryly taught at school. Rather, I am going to put you into the heART of the moment and kindly ask you to hear some words of my soul in gratitude to the art form of poetry, that quite frankly, saved my life. This poem along with other creatively healing poems can be found in my book, *Creative Locksmith: Helping You To Unlock Your Magic Within.* I sincerely hope these words can help you to think, feel, connect, or transcend in whatever way works for you. And if not, then feel free, be inspired to write your own words in a way that does work for you. As the saying goes, it is horses for courses!

A Gift of Words – Ode to Poetry

I owe you so much
for my soul is touched
and rescued by simple words
put into verse
that allow me to be heard.

My spiritual path imploded
my creativity exploded
you have given me your gift
to give others an uplift
to a wonderful place
both inner and outer space.

I know this is only the start
of many wisdoms to part
from my lips and my pen
to a wonderful time when
we will once again be
in the golden age.

I love this full creative flow
completely surrendered, my pen
does go wherever you send me
I know there is a message
everywhere I look, enough
to fill book after book!

And so the time has come to live my dream
and be everything I am, it seems
that I am reaping golden blessings,
following rehearsals
and many costume dressings,
finally I have returned to me
wise beautiful and soul free –
so thank you poetry for giving this treasure,
with pleasure to me and to thee
YO! Giving grateful applause for P-O-E-T-R-Y!

by Zoe Owl

Everyone has a story to tell. That includes you! You may be fortunate to have a joyful and positive story to tell, and if that is you then the world awaits your story in much need and anticipation to hear of it and to learn from you. Sharing your experience and wisdom is indeed caring. So what are you waiting for? Or perhaps like many of us that go through this transformational adventure called life, you may not like aspects of your story, or perhaps even big chapters of your journey, and be on a path that is seeking to change it, to transform your life in small or perhaps more drastic ways. The good news is you can and you have the complete freedom to do whatever you want and feel is right for you. You just need to give yourself the permission to do so! To re-write your script, making you the main character in your own show. Who in their clear state of mind would opt to be a stand-in or an extra, a background actor playing a minor role when you can choose to be the main lead character of your life? Step forward, you are your own life script writer, story teller, director and most central, main character. Your time has come, this is your play and your series of chapters, this is your life and your chance of being who you really are, in leading the life that you want to live. Women's coach and speaker, Felicity Okolo says in her book It Is My Life and I Am In Charge, *I love the unknown because I can make it into what I want it to be*, echoing, renaissance magicians like Ficino and Pico della Mirandola who famously wrote that we need to be the poets, writers and artists of our own lives.

Your audience awaits you.

Whether your audience is you yourself, because you are enough, or if your audience is your pet cat or your dog, your children, nuclear or wider family, friends, acquaintances and colleagues, your community or the wider world at large, it matters not. What matters is that you authentically express your truth of who you are. The story unfolding on the stage of your life, of how you want to be and how it will pan out, is largely within your control, so write, tell, direct and act well because this is it, no more dress rehearsals. We are now at the heART of the matter, and what matters only is YOU!

REFERENCES:

Dalebout, Katie (2016): Let It Out: A Journey Through Journalling, Hay House, USA. www.katiedaleabout.com

Ficino, Marsilio (1980): The Book Of Life. A fifteenth century book translated by Charles Boer. Spring Publications, Dallas.

Okolo, Felicity (2010): It Is My Life and I Am in Charge, Lightning Source UK Ltd., Milton Keynes, UK. www.felicityokolo.com

Owl, Zoë (2015): SOULutions: Soul Healing Poetry to Set your Soul Free. Createspace.com, USA. www.zoeowl.soulfree@facebook.com www.zoeowl.com

Owl, Zoë (2016): Creative Locksmith, Createspace.com, USA. www.zoeowl.com

Owl mandala

Get out of the House

Take a walk into another world

Laura

IT'S FAR-REACHING, the effect of taking an unexpected walk into a new energy and atmosphere. It's so easy to get caught up in the daily stuff of life, the mould we create and then feel obliged to shape and live out. I made a vow to myself that whenever Jason asks me out for a walk, I simply shut down my computer and go with him. That's because he has an amazing knack of taking me to the most beautiful nature spots in Sussex and I always feel so connected and re-energised from his wisdom walks that I return with a greater sense of love for what I am doing.

This is so throughout life, including in our thoughts. We are great at mindless self-sabotage and it can be so easy to slip into unhelpful thinking habits that really don't support us. Our minds are wired for infinite possibilities and we live in our small stories that limit what we take from life for us. Years of studying and teaching spiritual practices allow me to know fully that the power of setting a positive intention, believing in it as done and then leaving it be with love and *belief* is the only way to allow it to manifest. Be sure of what you command into your life, know how it already exists and see it in your life and in your mind's eye, imagine yourself living with it. Get out of the house within. Affirm what you claim for yourself and know that it's done already, it exists and is searching for you now. Would you tread mud all over the newly vacuumed cream hallway carpet? I don't think so! Same with your dreams and aspirations, you are visioning a new set of perceptions that need space to seed, root and grow. This can only happen with patience, commitment and certainty that *it's done* and there's nothing more for you to do. The power of letting go, in belief, is the power that can create miracles.

Below are a few different suggestions that you can use to diffuse unwanted thoughts.

You can...

- Go for an inner walk. Sit in a comfortable, calm space that is sacred to you and focus on the breath and on something nurturing for yourself. Shed any thoughts that pull your dreams down and instantly recreate the FEELING of what you wish to experience in your life. Make it good, make it your ultimate dream for your life and feel the feeling that you would have from this experience if you were living it right now. Focus only on the good in your life; create the feeling you want to experience and replicate that feeling within you. Capture it in your mind and heart and put energy into it.
- Be your own safety net. If in a moment of weakness you feel yourself slipping into an old *can't do* thought pattern – have a very positive affirmation at hand to say with meaning and know that it's DONE.
- Take a positive, tangible step of action towards your goal; this is great for letting life know you mean business – make that call, send the email, pack the travel bag, let life know you mean

action. Show life your devotion and commitment by taking daily positive action steps in the direction of where you're heading.

- Above all stay rooted in the NOW – love every second of this glorious life and the infinite possibilities here for you. Allow life in and enjoy it.

Action Woman

Taking action is a central part of creating your life, your way. Inner action involves giving yourself time to unravel and to be clear about your dreams and desires. Each author here knows that inner and outer action choices are vital for creating momentum in the physical world. As a metaphysical mama I've trained long and lovingly to know, for myself, that my inner world is my domain and the outer steps I choose to take are simply a continuum of momentum for my inner conviction. It's an art, and one that fascinates me as I study and learn how to use it more effectively for my life. I am the creative artist of my life and allow the channel to open for wondrous change.

Action is certainly not running around in desperation when the latest bill comes through the door or when your children go out and switch off their phones and panic sets into your heart!

Taking action is firstly connecting to the one all-good force of life and then making centred choices from this place of deep inner faith that all is happening for your highest good right now, whatever you feel about this particular obstacle and however hard it may seem to overcome. All is possible in life with faith, inner calm and inspired action. Breathe calmly, stay centered and grounded, always coming back to a place where you know in your heart that you are doing the very best you can right now in this situation. This is an extremely healing affirmation.

It's in the Way You Walk

THE LABYRINTH is the most fantastic tool for getting to know yourself! For those of you familiar with the gentle, winding circles that can be walked whilst contemplating your life, you are privy to the most enriching of tools for inner knowing. If you are new to the *Way of the Labyrinth* then allow your heart to open as you indulge on a walk that can literally change the way that you think about life.

Labyrinths are often mistaken for mazes, the main difference being that a labyrinth has no walls and there is simply one path that continues from beginning to end. Its ancient and mystical design is a sacred geometry that dates back at least 2500 years. At that time people would walk their yearly pilgrimage to the Holy Land, however during war and famine their route was often disrupted and so certain religious elders were intuited to create large spiral designs that could allow for contemplative walking in a safe space. These designs were always created In a similar way and used by thousands of people to meditate and reflect on their lives, so labyrinths were used initially as a religious tool. However over the centuries they have been designed, built and used by all people for all cultures, religions and races to allow for deeper contemplation. Labyrinths are so often refered to in the feminine due to the nature of the design, the opening being symbolic of the female form. The word *labya* means the inner and outer folds of the vulva. For me it is clear that the labyrinth is a tool created by the wise women, the spiritual leaders of that time, to embrace the feminine Earth Mother and Gaia and to allow for nature to come through with its meaningful messages. Our job as humans is simply to listen patiently and allow wisdom through whilst walking the path.

Just ONE journey on the labyrinth can open you up to insight and wisdom you would never dream of in everyday running around. My first labyrinth walk brought such transformation that it dynamically shifted my perspective on my life, allowing me to really let go of the old, heal it, forgive it and send it off to the unknown with love. From this place, the heart of the labyrinth, I invited in the new and wow, what a newness that is! I am the greatest advocate for walking the *Labyrinth's Way* and I invite you to seek out a labyrinth.

Nowadays too, you can find the most beautiful labyrinths all around the world, many old and many new, public and private and built in all settings from universities, such as Edinburgh, to wellness centres, prisons, parks and schools. Generally they are free to walk, unless you choose an organised group or workshop. Find your nearest labyrinth by going to this site: *www.worldwidelabyrinthlocator.com* or even easier, plant the seed of thought in your mind and you'll be guided to one through a conversation or the great plan of life itself.

Simple Guidelines for Labyrinth Walking

- Give yourself time to walk the labyrinth especially before and afterwards as you may wish to sit and contemplate your insights.
- Always walk the complete journey in SILENCE.
- Ask a poignant question as you enter and begin your walk, such as *Am I on my true path? How can I bring more love and peace into my life?*
- Whilst walking her path, listen deeply in the silence and know that any things that distract you while walking are your messages: there may be a bird singing just as you have a certain thought or a car passing during another.
- They are all messages for guidance, so stay open to it all.
- Keep your question and answers to yourself. This preserves the energy and allows for magic to happen.
- Allow time for contemplation afterwards; bring a journal if you feel you want to record your thoughts and feelings.
- Await your answer with patience. It may not arrive immediately so be open for the following days or weeks and allow your dreams to receive information and wisdom. It may come through conversation with another person, so be ready and open.

- Let go of asking *How?* Just allow things to unfold in the naturalness of time.

Freedom is Yours NOW

Recently I spoke with a client who expressed a feeling of 'trapped' in her life, impatient to reach the world that she is creating in her mind and frustrated that life just wasn't happening in the way that she felt it should. Of course, there are many times when this is what my life feels like too so I reflected on this for a while as it gave me the opportunity to see how I have worked through so much in the past four years. I used to live in a large sprawling home in the middle of the countryside but now I'm in a town house in a village and learning to negotiate space in many ways. When I first moved here I took a deep breath and thanked life for giving me warmth, shelter and a solid home to accomodate me, my family and my big life visions; that is certainly what it's doing as, living here, I am mastering the art of gratitude and embracing freedom. You see, there are always times when we can choose to feel as if life's dealt us the bad hand or that we feel constricted and squashed into a space that can't allow us to be free, to breathe easily and be who we are. These are the blessed times of growth and learning that no extra five bedrooms or separate utility room can ever teach us. When we feel like that, FREEDOM is always just around the corner. That's the time to look within, to understand that we firstly create a *feeling* of freedom and from there outer reality can only mirror it. Whatever you *feel* would bring you freedom, must firstly be loved and desired in your mind and from that point life can *only* bring it into your world. You can unlock the chains, from within and then witness your life unfold with love. Positive thinking is a part of this, but it's not the whole picture. We can always fake a smile or tell ourselves we are doing well when we really don't feel that way. What matters in the big mix is the FAITH and BELIEF that life is on your side, whatever is going on and that as you take a huge step from one stepping stone to the next, you are setting foot into the world of your dreams.

To change anything outside us there is one golden rule…

'Be that which you desire firstly in Mind. Create your sense and knowing of FREEDOM right where you are by being increasingly grateful, not quite satisfied, yet so thankful for who you are, for what you have, for all that

there is and for the wealth of creative flow that's just under the surface waiting for you to unleash to the world.'

Laura

And then It all begins – with you! We can lead you to the ocean of all that we are sharing here with you, but the next meaningful move is your stroke of willingness and action to swim out with LOVE and ACTION, like there's no tomorrow kind of action. You may know that feeling when you really, *really* want something and by hook or by crook you find a way to bring it into your world? Well that's what is needed here. A desire so strong that it creates shifts and changes which empower you to take charge of your life from the only place there is – within. So, go for it now! Don't wait. Enjoy yourself, let yourself have fun, experiment and most of all know that you are more than enough just as you are and your world awaits you with the fullness of love as a graceful, all powerful and confident loving *Mama on a Mission*, giving yourself permission to *SHINE.*

Sacred labyrinth mandala

Laura Topper

SoulFULL, positive, New Thought singer song-writer, recorded artist, founder of *Mama on a Mission*. Laura weaves together her deeper knowing of spirituality, metaphysics and life itself, gifting to the world her impactful healing songs and teachings.

Laura's world transformed on a dynamic labyrinth walk in 2012. She is now devoted 100% to uplifting beliefs in self love and abundance consciousness. Laura creates healing songs and chants that can allow for life transformation and shifts in thoughts, in the understanding that true change only happens when we allow thoughts and beliefs to move from our set limitations. Laura's straight to the heart albums *Now*, *The Gift*, *Metamorphosis* and *Divine Release* are reminders that by embracing positive messages and affirmations we can willingly choose to change our thoughts and beliefs to fill each moment with love, inner peace, abundance and JOY.

Contact Laura and listen to her songs: www.lauratopper.com

Mel Campbell

Mel was always drawn to self-discovery and finding one's inner purpose, which initially attracted her to the profession of occupational therapy some 25 years ago. With the birth of her first daughter, Mel was drawn to yoga and she embarked on a teacher training course to delve deeper into the practice. In 2003 Mel, her husband and two young daughters headed off to Thailand where Mel taught and studied yoga with diverse, skilled teachers soon realising that she was forever a student of herself. Here Mel discovered she was unexpectedly pregnant which inspired her to write her book *The Yoga of Pregnancy*, which embodies the physiology of changes to mother and baby through meditation, yoga and affirmations.

On returning to the UK, Mel reconfirmed her passion for occupational therapy, working with children and young people and is currently creating a yoga DVD to support her work in OT. A busy working mum to her three daughters, Mel now lives in a tranquil village just outside Brighton.

Contact Mel: yogawithmel.campbell@gmail.com

Patricias iris Kerins

Patricia Iris Kerins DHP, author of *The Magic of the Magdalene Key* is a clear channel for Source and the symbol of the Divine Christed Feminine Energy, Mary Magdalene. She is a spiritual teacher and TV/radio show presenter, popular motivational speaker, singer/songwriter, sound healer, as well as hypnotherapist and psychotherapist, *Viva Love* and *Voice Empowerment* life coach and workshop facilitator.

Patricia is currently working on the follow-up to her fiction novel *The Magic of the Magdalene Key* and a set of divination cards to accompany this, all downloaded from the Magdalene. Patricia's TV show airs every second Tuesday at 8pm, UK time, on the *Gift of Healing* TV platform and is called *The Patricia Iris Kerins Show.*

She lives near Loch Lomond in Scotland with her husband Bill and her little dog, Mr Murphy. She has been serving Spirit for over twenty-five years and loves her work which is all about LOVE.

Contact Patricia: www.patriciairiskerins.com twitter.com/patricia_iris,

patriciairiskerins@patriciairiskerins.com facebook.com/piksoulcoach

Belle Amatt

Belle's new novel, *Balloon Girl*, is a contemporary women's and teen fiction: a tale of motherhood, role-modelling and forgiveness

Belle also blogs and indulges in plenty of social media to inspire on-going good health. Her novels aim to offer fictional journeys which readers may relate to, empathise with and feel supported by. Belle has a BA in English Literature, a BSc in Nutritional Medicine from Thames Valley University as well as a background in teaching. These blend perfectly in offering sound nutritional knowledge and the motivation to push forward with healthy living. She offers nutrition based services include 1-1 consultations, food intolerance testing, workshops, *Cleanse* courses, lectures, menu creation, product reviews and articles on nutrition, food and lifestyle.

Belle lives in West Sussex with her partner, daughters and two cats. Days are spent mothering, nourishing, advising, lecturing, writing and hosting workshops.

Contact Belle: www.belleamatt.com

Twitter @BelleANutrition

www.facebook.com/BelleNutrition

Yvonne Skelly

Yvonne is dedicated to helping people live their lives in a heart centred way to bring more joy, happiness and fulfilment to their lives, allowing their true essence to emerge.

Yvonne, who hails from Dublin, Ireland, has over sixteen years experience in healing, with her own spiritual journey leading her to many healing modalities, including Reiki, *Rahanni Celestial Healing*, crystal healing and cranio-sacral therapy, to name but a few.

In 2011, Yvonne was intuitively guided to explore *Solfeggio Sound Healing* frequencies. She now blends these sacred sounds intuitively with other healing modalities. Each healing experience is a uniquc adventure based on what presents itself in that moment!

Yvonne also runs regular healing workshops, monthly full moon meditation, a monthly Women's Healing Circle, Divine Feminine Empowerment workshops, and she teaches Rahanni Celestial Healing. Yvonne is co-founder of **Naas Holistic Centre** and travels internationally offering healing.

Contact Yvonne: www.deohealing.com

Kate Bartram Brown

Kate teaches spiritual classes around the world. Her client list includes artists, business executives, media, TV and film personalities, medics, teachers and most importantly mothers. Anyone who is ready to be the best version of themselves finds Kate when they are motivated to make the changes.

Her global company **Mini Me Yoga** is highly successful and Kate has created global demand for her classes, sessions and speaking engagements.

Her background as an entrepreneur is recognised in the business world through being nominated for *Grazia's Business Woman of the Year*, featured on TV, magazines & newspapers for her achievements. She offers continued programs to help those who want to progress in their life, in which she supports them as they navigate day to day issues, business growth and advanced spiritual training.

Contact Kate: kate@minimeyoga.com

Zoë Owl

Zoë is an Inventive Creative and Lover of Life! Her mission is to create, empower and inspire others and in the process of having fun! She is most at home in nature, anywhere on Mother Earth but also loves living in London with her young son, Rory and their brother and sister black cats, aptly named 'Star' and 'Lite'. Becoming a mother simply changed her whole life and perspective for the better; and blossoming in her creativity whilst being of service to Spirit is the fun side of expressing her journey so far.

Zoë is an experienced psychologist, intuitive counsellor, psychotherapeutic hypnotherapist, NLP practitioner, *Past Life Regression* therapist, oracle card reader, Reiki workshop leader, performance poet and author. Zoë Owl's books, *SOULutions: soul healing poetry to set your soulf free* and *The Kids' Book of Wisdoms: on all kinds of stuff*, *Creative Locksmith, Goddess You* can all be purchased from www.createspace.com and www.amazon.com

Contact Zoë: Zoeowl.soulfree@facebook.com
Twitter @zoe_owl
www.zoeowl.com

MAMA ON A MISSION COMMUNITY

We welcome you to be a part of the growing
Mama on a Mission Global Community ~ join us at

www.facebook.com/groups/mamaonamissionglobalgathering/

The *Mama on a Mission* book is now available for you to sell in your business, bookshop, holistic centre or practice.

For wholesale enquiries and information about
Mama on a Mission workshops, events and circles
contact Laura at

treeofstrengthhealing@rocketmail.com

TREE OF STRENGTH

Glossary

BEING ENOUGH ~ You are a beautiful spark of life and this is enough. You can be you and more of you and live with love as your essence. This is enough, there is no need to prove anything to anyone.

CONNECT ~ To bring your awareness to the power of life, which is greater than all you can imagine, and know that this is the power that bought you here.

FAITH ~ Trust and belief that you have in yourself and the power of life.

FLOW ~ The force that is the all good ever-existent energy of life.

HIGHEST GOOD ~ Life wants the best for us and when we listen in silence from our heart and put aside our judgment we always know what is for our Highest Good. This is our soul's calling.

INNER CHILD ~ The part of us that remains our true essence, the voice within that gives us permission to connect with ourselves without inhibition, guilt or shame and just be who we are in that innocence.

INNER KNOWING ~ Your gut feeling, intuition, the inner voice that pushes and prods until you listen and act. All that you need already exists and the messages are always given to you as and when you are ready to look within and listen.

INTUITIVE VISIONING ~ A process that allows us to listen to the voice that is always here guiding us.

INVOCATION ~ To create a space and feeling that sets the scene for prayer and meditation. To open for Spirit's wisdom.

LABYRINTH ~ A spiralling pattern created in the ground that we can walk in silence and use the gentle turns to contemplate our life; some newer than others, they are located around the world and date back thousands of years.

SOUL ~ The doing part of us that takes and connects us to where we chose to be.

SOURCE ~ This is the infinite flow, power, energy and life force of all good that is always present, some know this as God, as Life, as Energy or as Unlimited Power.

SPIRIT ~ Life.

TRUTH ~ that there is only LOVE.

VISIONING ~ A meditational practice that opens us up to the answers through deeper listening.

VISUALISATION ~ The new story that we can replay in our mind using our creative imagination.

34992237R00175

Printed in Great Britain
by Amazon